STRESS MANAGEMENT TODAY

Jonathan C. Smith, PhD

To acquire the relaxation and meditation CDs designed for this book:
http://drsmith.deltalprinting.com

STRESS MANAGEMENT TODAY

COPYRIGHT STATEMENT

ISBN 1-4116-4068-3

WELCOME TO STRESS MANAGEMENT!

This book is part of a growing family of stress management tools that have come out of the labs at Chicago's Roosevelt University Stress Institute. Let me introduce the entire family.

For the general reader . . .

Stress Management Today is a practical guide for the general public, clients in therapy or counseling, and introductory college students. I have put together a full range of approaches generally recognized as safe and effective by health professionals, and have presented how-to instructions that are simple and to-the-point. **Stress Management Today** is not a professional text or scholarly tome. For accompanying recommended CD recordings of relaxation exercises, see: www.drsmith.deltalprinting.com

For professionals . . .

Health professionals, graduate students in the health professions, and professional trainers may be interested two essential professional textbooks: **Stress Management: A Comprehensive Handbook of Techniques and Strategies** and **Relaxation, Meditation, and Mindfulness: A Mental Heath Practitioner's Guide to New and Traditional Approaches**. Both books are carefully coordinated with the Book. Any instructor who assigns the Book to students or clients is strongly advised to acquire the professional texts for use as an advanced guide. They are published through Springer Publishing Company and can be purchased directly by clicking www.springerpub.com, any good on-line bookstore such as amazon.com, or any major full-service bookstore.

For scholars . . .

Advanced students and scholars interested in the research and intellectual foundations of the approaches we introduce are invited to read the **ABC Relaxation Training** series of professional texts. This series is published by and available from www.springerpub.com. Also, information on tests included in this book as well as recent work at the Roosevelt University Stress Institute can be explored by clicking www.roosevelt.edu/stress.

ABOUT THE AUTHOR

Dr. Jonathan C. Smith is a Licensed Clinical Psychologist, Distinguished Professor of Psychology at Chicago's Roosevelt University, and Founding Director of the Roosevelt University Stress Institute. He is author of 15 books and three dozen professional articles on stress, relaxation, and meditation. Dr. Smith has taught stress management, relaxation, and meditation to several thousand individuals and has served as consultant for government, business, and health organizations in the US, Canada, Spain, France, India, Algeria, and the Peoples Republic of China..

CONTENTS

PART I
THE STRESS MAP

CHAPTER 1
THE "QUICK FIX"

The facts are in – stress is big news. The headlines inform us that too much stress is bad for you and make you sick, interfere with work and school, and even contribute to early death. Unfortunately, we can't discount these somber stories as tabloid hype. Stress can be bad for you. The good news is that stress management works. Health professionals have carefully studied dozens, even hundreds of approaches that offer genuine hope.

The popular media has covered stress for many years. Although the today's talk show topic vary from day to day, ("Stress and Heart Disease," "Stress and Success," "Stress and Your Lover"), one question never seems to go away. For the 30 years I have taught and written about stress management, I am most often asked: "Is there a quick stress fix, a simple trick, a 'stress-buster.' Is there some special technique I can use anytime and anywhere?" This question seems to appear everywhere, in newspapers, magazines, and popular books. It's talked about on television, magazines, television, and radio. Of course, I suspect most who ask the question already know the answer: "No. There are no easy answers."

Stress can be managed, even solved. And the tools are available to everyone. However, it is important to restrain the urge to grab a single technique. Instead, experiment and explore many tools. The first and best type of tool is a working map of stress.

You know the saying, "knowledge is power " To this we can add, " Ignorance . . . is weakness." Knowledge of stress can make a real and direct difference in how effectively you can manage the problems in your life. Let me illustrate. Here's someone who is not well-informed, and doesn't deal with stress well.

Gil is 35, married with children, a college grad, and has been working in an accounting firm for ten years. He is stressed out. Gil's upset over the mountain of "busywork" his boss assigns every day. "This is for beginners, those who are less trained and experienced." Gil's day is filled with tension, frustration, and irritation. He frets that "This is my lot in life, I'm the one who gets the dirty work. I'm the one everyone complains to. I get the mistakes to fit. I do the weekend work when no one else will come in. Why me? It's in my genes." At the end of the day Gil is so worked up that his stomach is upset. He doesn't talk to his wife and two kids, and has trouble getting to sleep. One day Gil reads a magazine article on stress management that recommends a meditation "stress-buster" exercise. He tries meditating religiously at home for three weeks. It doesn't work.

Clearly, Gil is under stress. And his magazine article taught him something, a meditation exercise. But this didn't work because Gil lacked a full and effective understanding of stress. As a result, he failed to try some important options and tended to get stuck in dead end techniques that didn't work.. What was Gil missing? For starters, what is the cause of the problem? Unfair and excessive work? If this is it, then perhaps a sensible first step would be to assertively and frankly confront his boss about his workload. But that's not all. I wonder why Gil hasn't talked to his boss. From his comment "It's in my genes," I suspect he is resigned to his situation. Perhaps Gil should try a form of stress management that corrects such useless negative thinking. And Gil clearly needs something to help him cool off at the end of the day. Unfortunately, he doesn't realize that different approaches to relaxation work for different people, and meditation is among the most difficult approaches. Perhaps Gil should have tried some other types of relaxation, perhaps yoga, breathing, imagery, or even massage. And then why isn't Gil talking to his wife? What types of stress are involved here?

It should be clear that Gil would benefit from a more complete and effective understanding of stress. He could use a map to avoid stress dead ends and guide him through the forest.

CHAPTER 1 EXERCISES

1. Go to the internet and do a search. How many listings can you find for stress? How many for stress management? Browse through the first few pages. What topics are currently most popular. Put your responses on the following page.

2. Stress is always in the news. How many newspaper and magazine articles can you find on stress? Check the Table of Contents for this book. Which topics can you find discussed in newspapers and magazines? Stress and illness? Relaxation? Stress management? Conflict resolution. Crises and catastrophes? Anger management? School Stress? Job stress? Do a websearch and find out what stress-related topics seem to be most popular this year? Can you suggest why these topics seem to be particularly popular now?

TOPICS FOUND ON THE WEB

CHAPTER 2
STRESSOR WARNING SIGNS

Most people already have a stress map. Although it may be a bit outdated and frayed, it's a useful place to begin. Think of a recent stressful event in your life. What happened? What are all the important details? People often give answers like the following:

Last week my husband was supposed to pick me up at the store. He did not arrive. I was frustrated and irritated. This was stressful.

Yesterday I got my phone bill. It was twice what I expected! My stomach started hurting and I felt sick.

I'm getting married tomorrow. I'm anxious about this.

I was just diagnosed with HIV infection. I'm so stressed out I just can't study. My grades are hurting.

My job is killing me. I have to work at different times every week, sometimes in the day and sometimes in the evening. I can tell I'm under stress. My blood pressure is going up and I'm now on medication for it.

Each of these stories has one thing in common, a simple stress map. In each an outside or external situation or event is seen as causing or triggering some form of distress, an aroused physical symptom or negative emotion. Stressful situations or events are called **stressors**. The negative effects that are

stirred up are forms of **arousal / distress**. So our beginning stress map is very simple:

STRESSORS ➜ AROUSAL / DISTRESS

Understanding stressors and distress is the first step in developing a working map of stress. But a good map does more than show roads, rivers, and cities. It also has warning signs pointing to potential danger areas, for example, roads under construction or detours. If you were to travel on such risky roads you may well encounter actual warning signs, "slippery when wet," "men (or women) working," "deer crossing," and so on. When you see such a sign, you take action by slowing down, driving more carefully, or even reconsidering your journey.

In the same way, it is important to know the warning signs of serious stressors. These are signs that your stressor may be especially serious and that you need to consider taking action.

First, let's consider what is not generally a warning sign. Short or acute stressors do not have much destructive effect. Taking an exam, going for an interview, speaking in public, or fixing a flat tire are of short duration. They appear to improve your body's ability to fight off minor infections from cuts and scrapes. Such challenges may well help us live longer! But if you seem not to be getting over an acute stressor, consider the possibility that there are more hidden stressors present. Perhaps breaking up with the girlfriend is stressful because you've been divorced and alone for 10 years. Perhaps not getting the mortgage is stressful because your extended family can't stand living together in the tiny trailer. If short-term stressors seem to be having long-term effects, consider whether there are other warning signs. Stress experts (Segerstrom & Miller, 2004; Smith, 2002) have examined hundreds of scientific studies have identified four:

1. Is your Stressor <u>Unwanted</u>?

Imagine your job requires that you move to a different part of the country. Obviously, the stressfulness of this change depends partly on whether or not you wanted to move. Undesired events are more serious stressors than neutral or desired events. What makes an event unwanted?

Think about the one thing you don't want to happen in your life (other than your own serious illness or untimely demise). Most people would say that it is some type of loss, such a loss of a loved one or relative. Loss is a part of life. People lose their parents and loved ones, their jobs, their homes, and so on. When considering whether a stressor is serious, ask yourself how much loss is involved.

2. Is your Stressor <u>Chronic</u>?

A chronic stressor lasts (or has the potential of lasting) a long time. It is persistent, with few breaks or periods of relief. It can be a part of a chain of stressors, part of a "domino effect" of interconnected problems. Serious examples include: chronic illness (cancer, AIDS, heart disease), unemployment, living in a war-zone, and so on. Although these are very serious examples, they point to an important warning sign question: How long-lasting or chronic are the combined stressors in your life?

3. Is your Stressor <u>Uncontrollable</u>?

A stressor is worse if there is little or nothing you can do about it. Unemployment isn't so bad if you are going back to school to learn a new skill. AIDS is less stressful than it was in the 1980's because it can be effectively controlled with medications. Stressors that are realistically hopeless are most likely to be serious.

4. The Stressor Requires <u>Major Life Change</u>?

The effect of a stressor is made worse when it requires that you make serious changes in your life,

especially in your identity and social role. For example, living with and taking care of a parent may be a chronic and uncontrollable stressor. Your parent is aging, and will not get any younger. The stressor may involve serious loss. You can no longer do the things you used to do with your parent. However, stress is worsened if you have to change your life, for example, and quit your job for one that gives you more time to be with your parent. You may have to change your role, and perhaps see yourself as essentially a "live-in nurse" rather than a "work supervisor," "student," or even "independent."

The Stressor Inventory

How much stress are you under? Our first step in answering this question involves taking a look at the stressors in your life. Stressors add up. Getting a traffic ticket may be a hassle. Getting a ticket, missing the bus, and losing one's keys is worse. And imagine how much stress you would experience if you also caught a cold and had to pay an unexpected bill!

Two physicians, Thomas Holmes and Richard Rahe (1967) were among the first to think of how stressors accumulate. They created one of the first stress tests ever, *The Social Readjustment Rating Scale*. This tests consists of a list of 43 life events. Here are some examples:

- ❑ Death of spouse
- ❑ Divorce
- ❑ Personal injury or illness
- ❑ Marriage
- ❑ Son or daughter leaving home
- ❑ Change in residence
- ❑ Minor violations of the law

To obtain a stressor score, one simply adds up the number of events. Note that sometimes good events can be a source of stress. The key is to look at the four warning signs of each stressor event.

Researchers now question whether a single stress inventory can fit all people. It is more likely that everyone has his or her own possible inventory. Rather than take a generic test, like the Social Readjustment Rating Scale, I recommend considering your own list. One can think of special lists for parents, children, senior citizens, those in the armed forces, and so on. On the following page I've listed some of the stressors my students have reported. Do any fit you? Which might you add to the list?

PARTIAL STUDENT STRESSOR LIST

- ❑ Getting rejected by a desired school
- ❑ Getting a bad grade in an important class
- ❑ Finding a new girlfriend / boyfriend
- ❑ Breaking up with a girlfriend / boyfriend
- ❑ Finding a roommate
- ❑ Living with an irritating roommate
- ❑ Finding a place to study
- ❑ Not having enough money for classes
- ❑ Living away from home
- ❑ Partying vs. studying
- ❑ Balancing obligations of work, school, and friends

The Stressor Meter

We can summarize this chapter with a tool you can use to evaluate the warning signs and stress potential of any situation or event in your life. It's the Stressor Meter. Simply check how unwanted, chronic, and uncontrollable your stressor is. Indicate how much life change is involved Finally, estimate its overall stress level.

THE STRESSOR METER

	LO					HI
How Unwanted is it?	①	②	③	④	⑤	⑥
How Chronic is it?	①	②	③	④	⑤	⑥
How Uncontrollable is it?	①	②	③	④	⑤	⑥
How much Life Change is involved?	①	②	③	④	⑤	⑥
STRESSOR SCORE (estimate)	①	②	③	④	⑤	⑥

Here's a simple stressor. On a recent boat trip, Josh was playing cards on an outdoor table. He put a $20 bill on the table and the bill blew away. Clearly Josh didn't want this to happen, but the loss wasn't serious. Was this a chronic, long-lasting stressor with lots of ramifications? Not really. It was more of an acute, time-limited event. Is his predicament uncontrollable? Just a little, but not much. Josh had several options; he could ask his friends for money, phone his wife, or walk. Things were relatively under control. Any life changes required? None. In sum, Josh had a mild stressor, as indicated here:

JOSH LOSES $20

	LO					HI
How Unwanted is it?	■■■■	③	④	⑤	⑥	
How Chronic is it?	■	②	③	④	⑤	⑥
How Uncontrollable is it?	■	②	③	④	⑤	⑥
How much Life Change is involved?	■	②	③	④	⑤	⑥
STRESSOR SCORE (estimate)	■	②	③	④	⑤	⑥

Here's a more serious problem. Rose and Bill were planning to get married. Much preparation went into making this a big celebration. On the day of the marriage, everything was in order. All the guests were there with many gifts. The pastor was present. But there was a problem -- Bill had not arrived. Rose tried phoning him at his apartment, but there was no answer. She eventually got through to his roommate, Josh. Unfortunately, Josh did not know where Bill was, except that two days ago he had packed all his belongings, taken them to an undisclosed place, and left a check for next month's rent. Bill also left Josh a note: "Sorry, something came up and I may not be coming back soon. Love, Josh." Rose now not only faces a wedding disaster, but all the negative ramifications. How will she pay for it? What happened to Bill? Will she have to resign to living the life of a single woman? Here's Rose's rating:

THE WEDDING?

	LO					HI
How Unwanted is it?	■■■■■■■■■■■■					
How Chronic is it?	■■■■■■■■	⑤	⑥			
How Uncontrollable is it?	■■■■■	④	⑤	⑥		
How much Life Change is involved?	■■■■■■■■■	⑥				
STRESSOR SCORE (estimate)	■■■■■■■■■■■					

Rose is facing a serious stressor. It's unwanted. It's chronic because it's negative effects and ramifications may well be long-lasting. Although it seems uncontrollable, there are things Rose can and must do. The loss is large, especially if she must give up her marriage plans and she ends up living an unwanted single life. That consequence would also represent a significant life change. So, Rose estimated that her overall stressor score is high.

What would Rose's rating be if (a) her parents decide to pay for the wedding, (b) Bill sends Rose a letter saying that he's gay and has had a lover for 5 years, and (c) Rose decides to start over and move to Chicago and start school?

There's Hope!

If your Stressor Meter is high, that doesn't mean you're out of luck. It is a warning sign that you should do something effective about stress, and perhaps try the ideas in this book.

Most people can think of a friend or acquaintance who probably has a high Stressor Meter score, and isn't doing well. These are the unfortunate people who have more than their share of catastrophes, and are "taking it hard." Perhaps they look very unhappy. Perhaps their performance at work is suffering. Perhaps they are suddenly coming down with unexpected illnesses. I suspect these are individuals with poor stress management skills.

You may also know someone who has had a hefty dose of misfortune in life, has a high Stressor Meter score, and is doing just fine. They seem healthy, in relatively good spirits, and are surviving. I propose these individuals possess effective stress management skills.

CHAPTER 2 EXERCISES

1. Social Readjustment Rating Scale

Go to the internet and do a google search for the "Social Readjustment Rating Scale" by Holmes and Rahe. (The student version is OK) Take and score the test. Find a site that is willing to give you some indication of whether your score is low or high. Then evaluate how accurate the test is for you. What's wrong with it? How is it accurate? Does it get at the stressor variables mentioned in this chapter?

2. Your Stressors

In the following spaces, create your own stressor test. List all the potential stressors someone like you (your age, your job or level in school, marital status) might encounter. Then check the stressors you have actually experienced in the past six months. Give your guess as to whether you are experiencing a low, moderate, or high number of stressors.

❏ _____

❏ _____

❏ _____

❏ _____

❏ _____

❏ _____

❏ _____

❏ _____

❏ _____

❏ _____

❏ _____

❏ _____

❏ _____

❏ _____

❏ _____

❏ _____

❏ _____

❏ _____

❏ _____

3. Stressor Meter Practice

Here are some descriptions of stressors. Estimate a
Stressor Meter score for each.

JOSE FAILS THE FIRST QUIZ

Jose is a nursing student in a local junior college in
a large city. This is his first year and he is just
learning the ropes of college life. His first course,
Biology, is a bit tougher than he thought. College is
not the same as high school. And living away from
family for the first time in a big city offers many
temptations and distractions. Josh has been
attending all the classes, and doing the required
homework. However, he is apparently doing
something wrong. His first quiz grade was and F.

How would you evaluate the degree of stress associated
with this stressor? Of course, there are some facts you do
not know, so you will have to guess. You will quickly discover
that Josh's score will vary depending on the facts.

	LO					HI
How Unwanted is it?	①	②	③	④	⑤	⑥
How Chronic is it?	①	②	③	④	⑤	⑥
How Uncontrollable is it?	①	②	③	④	⑤	⑥
How much Life Change is involved?	①	②	③	④	⑤	⑥
STRESSOR SCORE (estimate)	①	②	③	④	⑤	⑥

JILL GOES TO COLLEGE

Jill has lived with her family for 18 years and is
moving across the country to start her
undergraduate work at a strict church-run college
in the middle of South Dakota. This is the first
time she has spent time away from home and away
from her high-school friends. And there was Jon,
her boyfriend-prospect who is going to a college far
away from Jill. Jill will have to pay her way through
college. She has no friends in her new town.

	LO					HI
How Unwanted is it?	①	②	③	④	⑤	⑥
How Chronic is it?	①	②	③	④	⑤	⑥
How Uncontrollable is it?	①	②	③	④	⑤	⑥
How much Life Change is involved?	①	②	③	④	⑤	⑥
STRESSOR SCORE (estimate)	①	②	③	④	⑤	⑥

4. Your Stressors

Describe the stressors you are currently experiencing.
Give a Stress Meter Score for each.

NAME YOUR STRESSOR:

	LO					HI
How Unwanted is it?	①	②	③	④	⑤	⑥
How Chronic is it?	①	②	③	④	⑤	⑥
How Uncontrollable is it?	①	②	③	④	⑤	⑥
How much Life Change is involved?	①	②	③	④	⑤	⑥
STRESSOR SCORE (estimate)	①	②	③	④	⑤	⑥

EXPLAIN YOUR RATINGS

NAME YOUR STRESSOR:

NAME YOUR STRESSOR:

	LO					HI
How Unwanted is it?	①	②	③	④	⑤	⑥
How Chronic is it?	①	②	③	④	⑤	⑥
How Uncontrollable is it?	①	②	③	④	⑤	⑥
How much Life Change is involved?	①	②	③	④	⑤	⑥
STRESSOR SCORE (estimate)	①	②	③	④	⑤	⑥

EXPLAIN YOUR RATINGS

	LO					HI
How Unwanted is it?	①	②	③	④	⑤	⑥
How Chronic is it?	①	②	③	④	⑤	⑥
How Uncontrollable is it?	①	②	③	④	⑤	⑥
How much Life Change is involved?	①	②	③	④	⑤	⑥
STRESSOR SCORE (estimate)	①	②	③	④	⑤	⑥

EXPLAIN YOUR RATINGS

NAME YOUR STRESSOR:

NAME YOUR STRESSOR:

	LO					HI
How Unwanted is it?	①	②	③	④	⑤	⑥
How Chronic is it?	①	②	③	④	⑤	⑥
How Uncontrollable is it?	①	②	③	④	⑤	⑥
How much Life Change is involved?	①	②	③	④	⑤	⑥
STRESSOR SCORE (estimate)	①	②	③	④	⑤	⑥

EXPLAIN YOUR RATINGS

	LO					HI
How Unwanted is it?	①	②	③	④	⑤	⑥
How Chronic is it?	①	②	③	④	⑤	⑥
How Uncontrollable is it?	①	②	③	④	⑤	⑥
How much Life Change is involved?	①	②	③	④	⑤	⑥
STRESSOR SCORE (estimate)	①	②	③	④	⑤	⑥

EXPLAIN YOUR RATINGS

5. What's your Overall Stressor Score?

Looking back at your answers to the previous exercise. what would you estimate your overall stressor score to be? Once gain, this is just an estimate, based on how you feel. Please explain why you gave yourself the above stressor score:

YOUR OVERALL STRESSOR SCORE (estimate)

LO					HI
①	②	③	④	⑤	⑥

EXPLANATION

CHAPTER 3
THE STRESS ENGINE

Bernie is a waiter at a small vegetarian restaurant. For the last few weeks, he has had problems at work:

> *I'm making a lot more mistakes when waiting orders. I forget orders or get them mixed up. I seem to be wasting lots of time asking customers to repeat themselves, or serving tables in the wrong order. I think I'm under lots of stress, and it's beginning to show at work.*

Mouna is a busy accountant with a medical problem. She's seeing a specialist about a persistent abdominal pain. Here is her account:

> *I get this stomach ache and queasiness about midday, and it lasts until bedtime. Sometimes I feel so bad, I have to take a break and just rest. My specialist says I have acid stomach, aggravated by excessive stress. She wants me to take time off and deal with my stress.*

Sid is an art student specializing in computer graphics at the local college. He also works full-time as a bartender. For the last year or so, he's had more than his share of colds. It seems that every three or four weeks be begins coughing and has to stay home. Sid started to worry about why catches so many colds, and finally visited the school doctor. He now suspects where his problems are coming from.

> *My doctor say's it's stress. Stress builds up in my body and eventually reduces my resistance, and I am more likely to catch a cold. Several colds a year.*

Each of these accounts has the same message: one of the first signs of stress is distress. And stress-related distress can appear as:

*   Illness and physical symptoms
*   Reduced effectiveness at work, school, sports, and home
*   Negative emotions -- frustration, anxiety, depression, and anger

This completes the second half of our beginning stress map.

STRESSORS ➜ AROUSAL / DISTRESS

In this Chapter 2 we discussed stressors. We now consider how stressors create symptoms of distress. Understanding ths remarkable process can give us powerful tools for detecting when we are under stress and what to do about it.

The Stress Engine

Have you ever met a superman, or superwoman? This is a serious question because people sometimes do acquire near superhuman powers. We encounter them every day. Think about a recent football game. Then game is near its end. Players are exhausted. If you were this exhausted, you would almost certainly plop yourself on a sofa and sleep. Amazingly football player finds the energy to run to the goalpost. Here's another example. A letter carrier fights off a barking dog. Suddenly she finds energy and endurance she didn't know she had. A camper lifts a tree that has fallen on a tent, trapping the family puppy. Although not a weightlifter, he easily lifts 100 pounds. You may well have heard of similar accounts of apparently miraculous strength and endurance -- and often they are accurate. Here's why.

Each of us has an automatic ability that awakens and energizes us for emergency action. This is the body's stress engine, which when revved up it can do remarkable things. Unfortunately, this same engine is often in "overdrive," running fast when we're doing nothing, and creating the symptoms of distress.

Physiologist Walter Cannon (1929) noted that our ancestors in the wild evolved an automatic life-saving ability called stress arousal or the **fight or flight response**. Ancient humans hardly had time to figure how to ready their bodies to fight off attacks from gorillas, bears, or hostile tribes. Other animals, even the dinosaurs, had this ability. One of the most successful products of evolution is the brain's stress engine and its ability to automatically, without thought or planning, bring about the fight or flight response.

Here's how the stress engine works. Deep within the brain is an almond-sized organ, the hypothalamus. This is the body's "stress trigger." When activated, it immediately and automatically sends signals through the a branch of the nervous system (called the sympathetic nervous system) to energize selected organs. This response occurs within seconds. The hypothalamus also triggers the adrenal glands above the kidneys to secrete stress energizing hormones, such as fast-acting adrenalin and the slow and long-lasting corticoids. This hormonal response is more sluggish and can last for days and weeks, prolonging the effects of stress even after a threat is long gone.

These are the mechanics of the stress engine, responsible for the fight or flight response. But just how does stress arousal prepare us?

- Whether you are a football player, a boxer, or simply a child chasing a runaway cat, it takes energy to deal with an emergency. We get our stress energy from fuels in our body. The

hypothalamus complies by triggering the liver to release, sugars, fats, cholesterol (yes, cholesterol is also a body fuel), and proteins, are release into the bloodstream.
- Whether fighting or fleeing, we need oxygen to "burn" fuel (including cholesterol) in a process called metabolism. To increase oxygen flow, the hypothalamus signals the lungs to breathe faster. And breathing passages in the lungs (bronchial tubes) expand to let in more air.
- Enriched with fuel and oxygen, blood must quicky and efficiently go to the muscles that will be doing the "fighting" or "fleeing." The heart beats more quickly, and more blood is pumped with each beat, blood pressure increases.
- The muscles responsible for vigorous activity must take in increased blood supplied by the heart.. Blood vessels to the heart and big muscles expand, providing more fuel to parts of the body that may be involved in emergency action. Tiny blood vessels to the skin, particularly the palms of the hands and the feet, constrict. Blood is not essential here for vigorous action. Hands feel cold and clammy.
- As we work hard to fight or flee, fuels are burned and body heat increases. Heat is carried away as we breathe more quickly and perspire.
- Functions not needed for emergency action are reduced: stomach and intestinal activity are limited, and blood flow to the stomach, kidneys, and intestines decrease.

In addition, secondary changes occur that enhance our mobilization for emergency action:

- The body prepares itself for possible injury. Surface blood vessels constrict, reducing the possibility of serious blood loss. Clotting substances are dumped into the blood stream, easing the formation of protective scar tissue.
- The immune system increases activity in anticipation of possible infection, or reduces activity to minimize the potentially damaging effects of over infection and conserve resources for fighting and fleeing.
- Natural pain killers, endorphins, are released by the brain, to help us keep on going in the face of considerable discomfort.
- And finally, the body readies itself for active involvement with the outside world. Pupils of the eye enlarge to let in more light and enhance vision, palms and feet become moist to increase grip and traction when running, and brain activity increases.

Three things about autonomic stress arousal are important to recognize. First, it is adaptive, supplying quick energy for fighting off or fleeing attack, quickly responding to unexpected physical assault, and so on. Second, it can have a delayed and prolonged effect, important for maintaining stress-fighting resources at a high level over the weeks. And third, the response is automatically integrated. All relevant body systems are energized together – heart, lungs, circulatory system, and so on. One does not have to plan for increased stress arousal, as one might deliberately prepare the proper stance for striking a golf ball, or running a race. In times of severe crisis, our ancestors in the jungle needed complete automatic, quick energy.

Distress: The Costs of Fight or Flight

People may think of stress as always negative. However, the fight-or-flight response can be very useful, even life saving. It provides quick energy for the football player catching a pass, the secretary who must prepare for an immediate emergency, and the jogger running from a dog in the park.

However, the fight-or-flight response can also be triggered by nonemergencies like alarm clocks, worries, negative emotions, interpersonal conflict, and excessive work. In such cases, stress energy increases and is not discharged through vigorous emergency action. Over days and weeks, stress arousal continues to rise, eventually contributing to distress on body organs and illness. In sum, short-term stress isn't particularly bad for you; however, chronic and uncontrollable stress clearly impacts health and well-being (Segerstrom & Miller, 2004)

It would take many books to describe how stress arousal, or excessive running of the stress engine, can contribute to distress, to symptoms, illness, and ineffectiveness at work, school, sports, and home. If you are interested in the details, check Table 3.1.

Table 3.1
The Costs of Chronic Fight or Flight Stress Arousal (Especially "warning sign" Stress – See Chapter 2)

Physical Symptoms and Illness

High blood pressure. The stress engine pumps up blood pressure so that more blood gets to muscles for emergency action. If this goes on nonstop, blood pressure remains continuously high, a serious medical condition.
Coronary disease. In coronary disease, cholesterol and fats clog the arteries; occasionally a blood clot may break away and create a blockage in the heart (causing a heart attack) or the brain (causing a stroke). The stress engine dumps more cholesterol and fat into the blood as "fuel," as well as blood-clotting substances to reduce excessive bleeding in case of injury. However, when prolonged these very same beneficial effects become problems.
Cancer. Many people have a few cancer cells floating through their bloodstream. However, a well-functioning immune system quickly cleans up the danger. Prolonged exposure to certain stress hormones suppresses the immune system, increasing the likelihood that cancer may take hold.
The common cold and influenza. The immune system helps us fight of and recover from a wide range of respiratory diseases. If suppressed by stress (see "Cancer" above), we are more likely to catch a cold or the flu, and our illness is more likely be prolonged.
Other disorders related to stressful wear and tear and immune system disruption. Just about every illness patients report to physicians can be influenced by stress-related immune impairment: AIDS, angina, asthma, back pain, bardycardia, cancer, cardiac arrhythmia, chemotherapy side effect, colitis, common cold, coronary heart disease, diabetes, gastrointestinal disorders, hypertension, hyperventilation, inflamation and infection, influenza, injury/healing, insomnia, irritable bowel syndrome, migraine headaches, multiple sclerosis, muscle cramps, myocardial infarction, nausea, peptic ulcer, psoriasis, Raynouds syndrome, spasmodic dysmenorrhea, tachycardia, and tinnitus.

Performance / Attention Problems

The strain of running the stress engine for long periods of time can shrink attention span, flexibility, and memory span and lead to forgetfulness, loss of concentration, confusion, and tendency to make mistakes. Our ability to work, study, perform at sports, or even deal with home issues can suffer.

Negative Emotions

Negative stress emotions include fear, anxiety, depression, feeling blue, anger, and irritation. All of these are exaggerated by worry. Although negative emotions are not a direct result of stress arousal, they are connected.

Is Your Stress Engine in Overdrive?

You can be unaware of stress arousal through a process called **habituation**. The brain can tune out constant, unchanging stimuli, whether it be the background drone of air conditioners, traffic noise – or stress. The signs of stress arousal can also habituate so that we become "numb" to or unaware of them. One important step of stress management is to recognize your distress / arousal symptoms. Generally, they fall into three categories:

- Worry, feeling distressed, anxious, fearful, irritated, angry, depressed, blue.
- Attention deficits (trouble concentrating, forgetfulness, being easily distracted, feeling confused)
- Stress-related physical symptoms

Researchers at the Roosevelt University Stress Institute have developed a simple stress test that can help you determine if you have excessive stress arousal. We have tried this test out on thousands of individuals, including several hundred college students. When asking if you are experiencing high levels of stress arousal, our test can be a useful starting point. However, keep in mind that a high score can mean many things, including an underlying medical condition (so you might consider seeing a physician if your scores are high). It is more likely that a high score is stress-related if you have a lot of stressors in your life (Chapter 2). The probability is even greater if any of the additional stress-enhancing behaviors described in the next chapter (for example, engaging in needless negative thinking, stirring up exaggerated feelings of arousal and upset, or do the wrong thing in an attempt to make stress better). More on that later. First, your stress arousal / distress level.

CHAPTER 3 EXERCISES

1. Measuring Stress Arousal / Distress

STRESS MANAGEMENT TODAY
STRESS TEST

To what extent do the following statements generally or typically fit you?
Please rate each item using the following key.

O	①	②	③
DOESN'T FIT	FITS ME A LITTLE	FITS ME MODERATELY	FITS ME VERY WELL

O ① ② ③   I worry too much about things that do not really matter.
O ① ② ③   I have difficulty controlling negative thoughts.
O ① ② ③   I feel distressed (discouraged or sad).
O ① ② ③   I am depressed.
O ① ② ③   I am anxious.
O ① ② ③   I have difficulty keeping troublesome thoughts out of mind.
O ① ② ③   I am afraid.
O ① ② ③   I find myself thinking unimportant, bothersome thoughts.
O ① ② ③   I feel irritated or angry.

_____   WHAT IS THE SUM OF YOUR RATINGS? THIS IS YOUR NEGATIVE EMOTION / WORRY SCORE.

O ① ② ③   I have nervous stomach.
O ① ② ③   I lose sleep.
O ① ② ③   My breathing is hurried, shallow, or uneven.
O ① ② ③   My heart beats fast, hard, or irregularly.
O ① ② ③   I lose my appetite.
O ① ② ③   My mouth feels dry.
O ① ② ③   I perspire or feel too warm.
O ① ② ③   I feel the need to go to the rest room unnecessarily.
O ① ② ③   I feel fatigued.
O ① ② ③   My shoulders, neck, or back are tense.
O ① ② ③   My muscles feel tight, tense, or clenched up (furrowed brow, tightened fist, clenched jaws).
O ① ② ③   I have backaches.
O ① ② ③   I have headaches.

_____   WHAT IS THE SUM OF YOUR RATINGS? THIS IS YOUR PHYSICAL SYMPTOMS SCORE.

O ① ② ③   I become easily distracted.
O ① ② ③   I lose my memory and forget things.
O ① ② ③   I feel confused.
O ① ② ③   I lose my concentration.
O ① ② ③   I feel disorganized.
O ① ② ③   I feel restless and fidgety.

_____   WHAT IS THE SUM OF YOUR RATINGS? THIS IS YOUR ATTENTION DEFICITS SCORE.

WHERE DO YOU FIT?

NEGATIVE EMOTION / WORRY

	Men	Women
High Stress	8-27	9-27
Medium	3-7	4-8
Low	0-2	0-3

PHYSICAL SYMPTOMS

	Men	Women
High Stress	9-39	9-39
Medium	4-8	5-8
Low	0-3	0-4

ATTENTION DEFICITS

	Men	Women
High Stress	7-18	6-18
Medium	4-6	3-5
Low	0-3	0-2

FOR NORM DATA: www.roosevelt.edu/stress

CHAPTER 4
STRESS BOOSTER BUTTONS

Hector is trying to relax using his new portable music player. He lies back in his comfortable sofa, inserts a CD, and pops on the earphones. Anticipating a wonderful serenade of beautiful songs, he switches his device on. Screech! He is assaulted with an ungodly blast of noise. Hector rips off the offending device.. He wonders "What's wrong? Why doesn't this CD player work? A bad CD? Maybe I should take the CD back to the store! Bad earphones? Maybe I should return them." Then he discovers the problem. He had brushed against three buttons on his music player — one for boosting volume, one for boosting the low booming sounds, and one for boosting the high pitched notes — all at once. The booster buttons caused the big screech!

It is easy to think of stress in simple cause-effect terms. It is tempting to conclude that an external stressor causes us to feel upset and distressed. At first Hector blamed the CD and his earphones. In stress situations we might blame our noisy child for our headaches, our insensitive coworkers for our work frustration, or our crazy schedules for our fatigue. In other words, stress is something like an arrow:

STRESSORS ➡ AROUSAL / DISTRESS

But if you think about it, there is something wrong with this simple cause-effect arrow. If things were that simple, our problems, although painful, would quickly pass. You might stub your toe on the steps (stressor) and feel stirred up and in pain (arousal / distress), and get over it. In reality, the world is much more complicated. Your boss may unfairly deny you a raise (stressor) and you get angry with an upset stomach (arousal / distress). But the story, of course, doesn't end here. You may worry. Work may suffer. You may start drinking, etc.

There is an very important missing part to our stress arrow. If you have ever tried one of the popular portable CD, MP3 players, or pocket radios, you are likely familiar with the many booster buttons that adorn their surface — a button for boosting the volume, a button for boosting the bass, a button for boosting sensitivity, and so on. Similarly, we can think of three **stress booster buttons** that crank up the severity and duration of both stressor and arousal / distress. We now look at these booster buttons and see how they point to three fundamental types of stress management. Specifically, here's how we can aggravate and prolong stress.

❶ We can **distort** stress with needless negative thinking,
❷ We can make **coping mistakes** in dealing with stress,
❸ Through our thoughts and coping attempts we can stir up exaggerated feelings of arousal and upset through a process called **self-stressing**.

Here's our improved stress arrow, complete with three new booster buttons. Let me describe how it works.

STRESSORS → AROUSAL / DISTRESS

❶ ❷ ❸
BOOSTER BUTTONS

In the following example Tony is facing a modest stressor and is experiencing some arousal / distress. However, he is boosting his problems three ways:

Tony is a beginning college student who has moved away from his mother to live in a college house. One weekend his mother called and announced that she was going to visit for two days. Tony became frustrated and upset because had other plans and wanted to be alone. So far we have a simple cause-effect stress arrow. MOTHER ANNOUNCES HER VISIT → TONY GETS UPSET.

*However, there's more to the story. Immediately after the call, Tony started thinking "She's checking up on me. Mother doesn't trust me. She always treats me like a child." Actually, this was a bit of an exaggeration, a **distortion**. In addition, Tony started thinking about how awful it is when his mother visits. He clenched his fists and held his breath. Tony was stirring himself up through **self-stressing**. And not wanting to be bothered, he yelled at his roommate not to bother him, probably a **coping mistake** in this situation.*

In sum, Tony aggravated and probably prolonged his stress through a bit or distorted thinking, stirring up feelings of upset, and not coping well. We now consider each stress booster

STRESS BOOSTER ❶ Distorting Stress

Here are two items from the famous stressor test, the Social Readjustment Rating Scale invented by Holmes and Rahe:

Going to Jail
Divorce

How we think about stressors influences their impact. When we distort our stressors, we often make them worse. Consider these two unfortunate people who had to spend a night in jail (because of too many parking tickets):

Inmate 1: *I can't stand being in jail. This seems like forever.*
Inmate 2: *It's only one night. I can take it. I'll get my life in order starting tomorrow.*

Or consider these two divorcees:

Divorcee 1: *Divorce is a personal failure. I simply do not have what it takes to get along with others. No one will ever want to date me again.*
Divorcee 2: *This divorce is unfortunate, but a challenge. I will have to learn from my mistakes. People who have been through marriage once are more mature, and better candidates for good marriage.*

It should be clear that our stressed out inmate and divorce are distorting their predicament by needlessly catastrophizing, personalizing, and assuming things will always be bad. Our less stressed examples are treating their situation as a challenging problem, not a catastrophe, and are generally cool-headed, realistic, and practical about their situation.

STRESS BOOSTER ❷ Coping Mistakes

There is no end to the specific mistakes people can make when attempting to cope with the problems of living. However, it is useful to view stressors as problems waiting to be solved. In this context, one can make several general types of mistakes:

• Denying and avoiding the situation

John has graduated from college and moved to a new city. He is living with friends and looking for a job as a cashier in a restaurant. Having little luck, he thinks *"I'll just hang around. Something will turn up. Things have a way of working out." Unfortunately, this line of thinking leads John to avoid looking for a job, thus increasing his stress.*

- Not looking at the real problem

Maria has made an agreement with her husband Jose. They are to take turns cleaning house every other week. Two weeks have gone by, dirt is piling up, and Jose hasn't touched the broom. Maria decides that if she doesn't clean on her week, Jose will think she doesn't love him. So she figures out how to spend an extra afternoon cleaning house. Clearly, the problem is not how to keep Jose's love, or even how to schedule extra cleaning time. Maria probably wants Jose to keep his side word and needs to deal with this.

- Getting stuck on one possible solution and not generating others

Roberta is trying to figure out the best way to meet guys. After school, she sits in her room with a pad of paper and decides to make a list. The first thing that comes to mind is "Call my friend Amy. She'll help me out. She always does!" Roberta runs to the phone and makes her call.

STRESS BOOSTER ❸ Self-Stressing

Let us return to the stress engine, fight or flight. Picture an unlucky distant ancestor, whom we shall name Tena. Tena encounters an angry bear in the forest. In response to this perceived threat, she experiences a quick rush of energy. As we have seen, her hypothalamus initiates a series of body changes that provide blood and oxygen to organs for vigorous action. In addition, through her attempts to cope and think about her dilemma, Tena boosts her stress energy through physical and mental **self-stressing**.

Physical Self-Stressing

Tena leaps into action and in an instant is ready for action. If this were a video, we could slow down the action and notice that she is engaging in three types of physical self-stressing

Stressed posture. Tena assumes a physical posture of readiness for fight or flight. She crouches in a defensive position and holds her arms still so not to upset the bear. **Stressed muscles.** Her muscles tighten, ready to run or flee at a moment's notice.

Stressed breathing. She holds her breath tightly, breathes in through her expanded chest, and takes an occasional deep sigh.

Mental Self-Stressing

Our ancestor continues to boost her stress level with her thoughts. The attacking bear jumps behind a bush. Tena knows she may have a battle on her hands, and tightens her stomach in determined anger. Inside she feels the energy burn. She pictures herself attacking the bear and feels her heart beat hard as her fear and anger increases. And she strains to attend to the hiding bear, looking behind several bushes, and thinking about several possible escape paths. Here we see three forms of mental self-stressing that can also rev up and prolong the fight or flight response.

Stressed body focus. Just attending to part of your body can create stress there. Years ago I discovered this ability to create body stress in a rather awkward encounter with my parents.

I was 14 and had just returned from a camping trip with my friends. Mom and dad were very interested in my adventures, until I described how we all came down with an itchy case of forest fleas! The entire camping group was miserable for a week. I then noticed that both of my parents were very silent. Dad started scratching the back of his head. After a long pause, I realized what I had done and reassured them that the entire group had completely eradicated the flea infection. We all laughed. Dad explained how just paying attention to the back of his head (with fleas on his mind) was enough to get his skin itching.

I hope this example hasn't got you itching! More seriously, when we think and fantasize about stressful encounters, we might focus on what we are doing physically, or what's happening in our bodies.

Here are examples of body focused thoughts:

I'm just about to sing in front of my church group. Gosh, I notice how warm I am inside. This upsets me. I hope no one notices.

In a few minutes I see my dentist. I'm nervously waiting in the reception area. I notice my stomach rumbling. I can feel it sinking. I feel queasy.

I've just made a date over the internet and am sitting in the coffee shop for our first encounter. I can almost hear my heart beating. Boy, it's beating fast!

I'm driving to work on the expressway and some fool just turned in front of me without signaling. I feel like yelling at him. I notice myself beginning to sweat. I feel like punching him.

In each of these examples, can you see when the person directed focus to a body sensation, such as physical warmth, the stomach, heartbeat, or perspiring? Such body-directed thoughts may further evoke fight or flight symptoms, especially in the "gut" or abdomen, and heart. We may experience queasy, sinking, or empty feelings in the stomach, a rapidly beating heart, or feeling flushed and warm. This is illustrated more fully below:

I imagine myself giving a big speech to my business group. In my mind I picture all the people in front of me quietly waiting for me to start talking. I imagine my hands shaking a little. I notice my heart beating hard. I feel queasy. I begin to sweat and feel warm as I think about all the people in front of me. I wonder if they will notice how nervous I am and my heart beats harder. Deep inside I have a sinking sensation. I perspire even more Then it hits me — I'm creating all these symptoms just by worrying about my big speech! The thoughts and mental pictures did a number on me! You can really worry yourself sick!

Stressed emotion. Psychologists frequently mention three types of negative feelings: anxiety and fear, irritation and anger, and depression and feeling blue. Most people can stir up these feelings if they choose to dwell on a negative thoughts that involve negative emotions. These thoughts include images, fantasies, and charged up words related to a stressor (anxious, angry, or depressed thoughts). Stressful emotions can augment the fight or flight response and color our experience of stressors.

Stressed attention. We can self-stress by straining to stay focused on a task; dividing attention through multitasking or doing several difficult things at once; thinking about both a stressor and preoccupations with worrisome thoughts or emotions.

Self-stressing has its place. Sometimes we encounter emergencies that require high levels of stress arousal. In such situations we learn to put up with associated distress. Such extreme situations may include engaging in vigorous sports, escaping an attacking animal, dealing with a prolonged highway emergency, and so on. In addition, we can experience self-stressing in less extreme situations, as illustrated in these examples:

Yoshi is a Junior in college and is having trouble getting into the college routine. She enjoyed her Summer vacation and is reluctant to get back to work. Unfortunately, Yoshi failed her English midterm. This really shook her up. The night after the midterm, she goes to the library, finds a good firm chair, and sits alert and upright **(stressful posture)**. *With pencil clenched in hand, brow furrowed, and jaws clenched, she opens her book* **(stressed muscles)** . *After a few deep breaths, she begins studying* **(stressed breathing)**. *From time to time Yoshi pauses to get herself motivated to continue with along night of study. She thinks about that awful moment she got her midterm back, and how her stomach churned and hands grew cold when she saw her grade. She gets "sick" just thinking about it, and thinking about her churning insides* **(stressed body focus)**. *Yoshi fearfully imagines the frown on her professors face as he reviews the correct answers. She repeats to herself how much she dislikes the professor, and feels a bit angry.* **(stressed emotion)**. *She attends to several tasks at once, calling her family on her cell phone while reading her textbook and trying to find her homework (multitasking); her attention is strenuously focused on the urgent task at hand., as well as on worries about what might go wrong and what she should do* **(stressed attention)**.

Here is another example:

Hector is a young legal assistant in a large law firm. Recently coworker Josh has been publically putting him down. Hector is a bit shy, but feels upset and intimidated every time Josh jokes about his hair, clothing choice, and preference for hats. One evening, Hector finds himself thinking about Josh's most recent insult. and decides to have a heart-to-heart talk. Because he sometimes has difficulty confronting others, Hector decides to practice what he is going to say. Alone at home, he stands, looks straight ahead, and folds his arms **(stressful posture)**. *He carefully furrows his brow, lowers his voice, and lifts his hands for emphasis* **(stressed muscles)**. *He takes a deep breath, hold it a little, and then breathes in a very careful, controlled way* **(stressed breathing)**. *He imagines the feelings of frustration and determination deep in his gut. He feels a sinking, empty sensation in his stomach, he thinks about his clenching, and his face feels a little warm* **(stressed body focus)**. *Then Hector rehearses in his mind what he is going to say, and begins to feel the irritation build* **(stressed emotion)**. *During the entire rehearsal exercise, is mind is truly full. He* *is focusing on what he should say and should not say, how he looks, and what might go wrong* (**stressed attention**).

CONNECTED BOOSTER BUTTONS

If you think about the three stress booster buttons, you may discover something very important. They are connected. For example, imagine you prepare for a long stressful hike by jumping up and down a few times. This coping preparatory strategy also tenses up your muscles (self-stressing) for the walk. How you cope may also be a form of self-stressing. When worrying about a low grade on a quiz, you may engage in exaggerated worry and think that this is the end of the world. Here distorting your situation can also be a type of self-stressing in which you stir up additional negative emotion and fear in yourself.

When thinking about stress, consider what you are thinking and doing. Then ask yourself if your thoughts and actions involve:

- Making any coping mistakes
- Distorting your situation
- Self-stressing

Here is how one student identified her stress booster buttons:

I just graduated from high school and am starting college in a town hundreds of miles away from home. I'm lonely, homesick, and a little frightened about my situation. Sometimes I stay in my dorm room all by myself and get depressed. I worry about how terrible my catastrophic situation is. This doesn't do any good (it's a coping mistake – I should be meeting other people in the dorm). I'm distorting things (realistically my situation is a challenge that is a little scary, not a terrible catastrophe). And it just makes me more anxious and depressed (self-stressed emotion).

CHAPTER 4 EXERCISES

1. Stressors: The Social Readjustment Rating Scale Revisited.

Recall from Chapter 2 that early stress researchers defined stress in terms of the Social Readjustment Rating Scale. What's wrong with using this as our only way of defining stress? Go to the internet and to a google search for "Social Readjustment Rating Scale." You will find many stress sites. Find a site that misuses this scale; explain what the site says, and how it is distorted.

```
┌──────────────────────────────────────┐
│ I FOUND THIS SITE                    │
│                                      │
│ WWW. _____ │
│                                      │
│ WHAT IT CLAIMS / MY ASSESSMENT       │
│                                      │
│                                      │
│                                      │
│                                      │
│                                      │
│                                      │
│                                      │
│                                      │
│                                      │
│                                      │
│                                      │
│                                      │
│                                      │
│                                      │
│                                      │
│                                      │
└──────────────────────────────────────┘
```

CHAPTER 5
TYPES OF STRESS MANAGEMENT

The stress management toolbox is overflowing. If you search the internet for stress management you will quickly uncover a never ending list, with "hits" ranging from acupuncture to Zen. Where does one begin? Actually, if you have read the first part of this book, or even the preceding page of text, you already know the answer.

There are three things we do to boost and prolong stress:

1. Distort stress through unrealistic thinking
2. Do the wrong thing through maladaptive coping
3. Stir up tension and feelings through self-stressing

These point to three general categories of stress management:

1. Thinking realistically
2. Coping effectively
3. Learning to relax

Three Types of Stress Management

There are three types of stress management. Thinking realistically not only reduces stress, but helps us relax. Learning to relax can help us think realistically. And learning to cope can influence both how realistically we think and our ability to relax.

Realistic Thinking

Needless distorted thinking makes stress worse. Realistic thinking involves catching ourselves in the act of thinking negatively, identifying and challenging our unrealistic thoughts, and figuring out what is more realistic. We see this illustrated here:

Sergio promised to take his friend Josh out to dinner on his birthday. Sergio forgot and felt terrible. At first, he started putting himself down with such negative thoughts as "I'm a worthless friend. No one can trust me." Then he came to his senses, and realized what he was saying to himself. "Gosh, I'm really doing a number on myself. Worthless? Untrustworthy? These are extreme words!" He took a deep breath, and rethought the situation. "Well, I shouldn't call myself worthless and untrustworthy. I was just very careless and perhaps sloppy for not putting Josh's birthday in my calendar." And he figured out a more realistic way of thinking. "I care for Josh and will take him out when he wants, maybe even twice. He's worth something to me, and I know him well enough that he thinks I'm worth something, otherwise he wouldn't spend time with me."

Such rethinking is easier said than done, and in following chapters we will look at a variety of powerful strategies for breaking bad negative thinking habits and approaching problems more effectively.

Effective Problem-Solving

There are many ways of doing nothing. One might pretend ("The problem will just go away on its own"), put things off ("I'll do it tomorrow, or the day after"), or even feign helplessness ("This is just to big for me. I'll just give up"). Problem-solving involves taking a realistic piece of a problem, identifying what one really wants, brainstorming options, and taking action. For example:

> *Kathy has just moved to a new town and is staying with a friend. She finally found a job and feels she must leave. But living with her friend is so easy. And because Kathy has never lived alone before, finding a place seems overwhelming. So one day she decides to get down to business and move. That evening, she goes to a local coffee house and lists what seems like realistic steps. How much rent can she afford? What neighborhoods does she like? How will she get to them? And most important, where can she call for help? She then proceeds with each question.*

The key to problem-solving is to accept that all parts of a problem can't be solved at once, and there may be many courses of action one could take. One then targets what can be solved.

Relaxation

When we self-stress we create for ourselves arousal and distress. Relaxation involves just the opposite, reducing arousal and distress. We will learn in our chapters on relaxation that each form of self-stressing has a corresponding relaxation family. This is shown in the table below.

Self-Stressing and Relaxation Techniques

Self-Stressing	Relaxation Technique
Physical	
• Stressed posture	• Yoga stretching
• Stressed muscles	• Progressive Muscle relaxation
• Stressed breathing	• Breathing relaxation techniques
Mental	
• Stressed body focus	• Relaxing body suggestions (Autogenic suggestion)
• Stressed emotion	• Relaxing imagery/Thoughts
• Stressed attention	• Meditation / Mindfulness

The Importance of Knowing the Map

Yes, the world of stress management is a jungle. Most people stumble from one technique to another until they hopefully find something that works. This is like traveling in a strange part of the country without a map. I believe it is important to know where you might be going and where you have been. At the very least, our map of stress management offers an overall bit of general advice:

When under stress, think realistically. Treat your stress as a problem-to-be-solved. And relax, replacing needless worry and self-generated upset with a clear focus on the task of the moment. This is the journey we will take in the remaining chapters.

CHAPTER 6
STRESS RESOURCES:
SOCIAL SUPPORT AND MEANING

Recently a distraught, single, and non-churchgoing student presented me with a disturbing article. The headline proclaimed:

> **MARRIED PEOPLE LIVE LONGER**
> **CHURCH-GOERS LIVE LONGER**
>
> ***GET MARRIED ! GO TO CHURCH!***

I have encountered the same message a number of times in the popular press. Such headlines are very misleading. Bad marriages can increase stress and illness. And those who belong to fundamentalistic and judgmental religious groups often have shorter lives.

The important facts are that *social support* and one's *beliefs* are associated with lower levels of stress. One can find social support in and out of marriage, and churches obviously are not the only source of meaning in life. Social support and meaning are two major stress resources, resources that can be tapped in part by using the tools and strategies of this book.

Social Support

Experts identify three types of social support: tangible, emotional, and information. People who offer tangible support provide physical help, such as:

- Sharing work in completing a job
- Money when needed
- Use of their car or cell phone
- A place to stay
- Food
- Babysitting
- A pencil during an exam

Emotional support involves showing care and acceptance as well as providing a listening ear to others. One does so without judgement or ulterior motive. When someone offers you emotional social support, you are more likely to think:

- "This person accepts me for who I am, regardless of what I've done or what I feel."
- "I can really open up to this person and share my feelings."

- "I don't have to worry about making a good impression or being judged or evaluated."
- "My friend takes time to listen, and doesn't preach or lecture me."
- "This person seems to know what I'm feeling and knows what its like to be in my shoes."

Information support involves useful instruction, facts, advice, and feedback, for example:

- Giving directions
- Explaining where to get help
- Showing how to do something
- Practicing ahead of time dealing with potentially stressful situations, such as giving a speech, interviewing for a job, asking someone out for a first date
- Giving feedback as to one's appearance, behavior, etc.

Social support can at times directly prevent stress or at least buffer the effects of stress. Social support can contribute to one's sense of being cared for, the feeling of belonging to a community, companionship and love, and the availability of help in times of trouble. Most important, people with a health social ties are heather and live longer than those without these ties. Numerous studies strongly support this conclusion, regardless of socio-economic status, race, gender, or general health (Karren, Hafen, Smith, & Frandsen, 2001).

The Meaning of It All

Both personal spirituality and commitment to organized religion can provide sources of hope, strength, and comfort beyond social support. Spirituality and religion sometimes involves, and at times does not involve, the idea of a personal God. In fact there are people who find deep meaning in life who do not believe in a personal God, and there are those who do believe in such a God who live stressful lives with little meaning. Let's begin by focusing on a tangible concern: meaning.

What is more important than your personal concerns, pleasures, and frustrations? What tells you to "keep on going" even when you are about to give up? Why take the time and effort to keep healthy, go to school, and learn stress management skills? These are the "deep meaning questions" of life. Sometimes, our first answers to such questions are somewhat restricted, for example:

I want to perfect my coping skills in order to be healthier.

Limited answers are important, but partial. Why do you want to be healthier? Eventually, if you keep asking "Why do this?" you encounter a deep meaning question, a justification for your choices and actions that is larger and more important than yourself. This is a *meaning resource*. Your meaning resource is your answer to such questions as:

- What in life is larger and more important than yourself?
- What bigger direction or purpose justifies doing things you might find temporarily frustrating or uncomfortable.
- Why bother resisting the immediate gratification of short-term pleasure, (including addiction and compulsion) procrastination, and inaction?

Of course, there is no one answer that is right for everyone. Here are a few students have shared:

- God wants me to be happy and productive.
- I am here to make the world a better and more loving place.
- Right now, I need to grow.

CHAPTER 6 EXERCISES

1. Social Support in Your Life

What are the sources of tangible support in your life? What types of tangible support might you expect?

Describe a situation in which you received tangible, emotional, or informational social support.

What are your sources of emotional social support?

What are your sources of informational social support?

2. Social Support Room (Adapted from Blonna, 2005)

Imagine the box below is a room. In this room is a chair reserved for you. Who are your sources of social support? Place as many additional chairs as you want in this room, one for each of these people. Indicate on each chair whether the person provides tangible, emotional, or informational support (label the chairs "T," "E," "I," or any combination). IF A PERSON IS A VERY IMPORTANT SOURCE OF SOCIAL SUPPORT, PLACE THEIR CHAIR VERY CLOSE TO YOUR CHAIR. IF THEIR SUPPORT ISN'T SO IMPORTANT, OR IS UNCERTAIN, PLACE THE CHAIR FARTHER AWAY. If you are not completely sure of what kind of support they can give, put a question mark by their chair.

YOUR SOCIAL SUPPORT ROOM

YOU

What are sources of deep meaning in your life? Place this as a candle in your room. Give it a label. This is your "meaning icon." If this is also a source of meaning for others in your room, connect the candle with their chairs (the lines from the candle are "rays of light" shining on you and others.

2. You as a Support-Giver

In this exercise, return to your social support room. Include all of the people you introduced in the room on the previous page. This time indicate to what extent you have offered tangible, informational, or emotional social support to each person. draw arrows from you pointing to each person to whom you have offered support in past. Label each arrow "T," "I," and/or "E" if you to indicate the type of support you have given.

YOUR SOCIAL SUPPORT AND MEANING ROOM

Now, include your meaning icon. Draw and arrow from yourself to your meaning icon indicating the degree to which you have actively incorporated it in your life. That is, if your source of meaning is something that gives you daily strength, meaning, and direction, make the arrow very strong. If your source of meaning is something you don't think about very much, but it's there in case you might need it in the future, make your arrow less heavy.

CHAPTER 7
YOUR STRESS DIARY

Are you under stress? We have seen that there can be a short answer and a more complete answer. You are under stress if you can identify a stressor and are experiencing stress arousal and distress. We see this in the following example:

Gosh, I'm under a lot of stress. My job just reassigned me to a different city and I will have to move. This has got me really nervous.

STRESSOR: *Job reassignment*
AROUSAL / DISTRESS: *Nervous*

The longer answer notes how coping mistakes, distorted thinking, and self-stressing contributes to stress, as illustrated here:

Gosh, I'm under a lot of stress. My job just reassigned me to a different city and I will have to move. This has got me really nervous. This couldn't have come at a worse time. I just moved out a rented house and bought a place. Maybe I should have waited. This could be a catastrophe, given that I'm completely helpless. I spend hours brooding about what might go wrong. This gets me all stirred up.

STRESSOR: *Job reassignment*
AROUSAL / DISTRESS: *Nervous*
COPING MISTAKE: *Buying a house*
DISTORTED THINKING: *Catastrophizing*
SELF-STRESSING: *Brooding*

Thus, when someone asks you if you are under stress, you can reply: "Here's the short answer . . ." or   "Here's the long answer . . ."

If you are reading this book as part of a stress-management program or course, or are personally committed to do as much as you can about stress in your life, I recommend completing the daily stress and coping diary and the end of this book. This diary will help you understand more about stress in your life and apply the strategies of this book.

Each page in your diary is similar to the "long answer" we described above. Here's what you include:

1.   TODAY'S STRESSOR: Name your day's most significant stressor.
2.   AROUSAL/DISTRESS: Did it disturb you? Describe your types and levels of arousal and distress.

For example, Jasdeep recently had a problem with his boss at the children's home.

TODAY'S MOST SIGNIFICANT STRESSOR
My boss criticized my monthly report.
AROUSAL / DISTRESS
I thought it was really good. He hated it. I felt stupid and pissed.

People often make a mistake when describing their "arousal / distress." The following examples show the mistake clearly:

```
     TODAY'S MOST SIGNIFICANT STRESSOR

I was late at work.

              AROUSAL / DISTRESS

I arrived and my boss stared at me very
critically.
```

```
     TODAY'S MOST SIGNIFICANT STRESSOR

I got into an argument with my spouse.

              AROUSAL / DISTRESS

My spouse forgot to order pizza for the
party tonight.
```

```
     TODAY'S MOST SIGNIFICANT STRESSOR

My doctor told me I had fractured my
wrist while skating.

              AROUSAL / DISTRESS

I am such a clumsy skater!
```

Notice that each example of arousal / distress is actually an elaboration of the stressor. Remember: arousal distress is always a feeling (like anxiety, fear, depression, sadness, anger, irritation) or a physical symptom. Here are these examples rewritten correctly.

```
     TODAY'S MOST SIGNIFICANT STRESSOR

I was late at work.  I arrived and my
boss stared at me very critically.

              AROUSAL / DISTRESS

I felt like a fool.  I was so
embarrassed!
```

```
     TODAY'S MOST SIGNIFICANT STRESSOR

I got into an argument with my spouse. My
spouse forgot to order pizza for the
party tonight.

              AROUSAL / DISTRESS

Boy was I furious!  I could have a cow!
```

```
     TODAY'S MOST SIGNIFICANT STRESSOR

My doctor told me I had fractured my
wrist while skating.

              AROUSAL / DISTRESS

I felt sheepish and upset.
```

After describing your stressor and arousal/distress, elaborate on the details of what happened. Here is where you tell the complete story of today's most significant stressor. Include where you were, when it happened, who was involved, exactly what happened, and most important, **what did you think and do to cope?** Here's Jasdeep:

```
   WHAT HAPPENED? DESCRIBE WHAT YOU
              THOUGHT AND DID
   THAT MADE THINGS BETTER OR WORSE.


Where were you?
When did this happen?
Who was involved?
What happened?

It was Friday afternoon, time to turn in
my weekly report in the daycare center.
I went into the boss's office, handed her
my one-page summary of what happened.  I
described any problems that came up.  She
looked at the report, closed her eyes,
sighed, and said "This isn't enough."  I
thought "I'm so stupid!  Can't I get
anything right.  This job is a disaster
for me."  I just sat there and took it
in.
```

Finally, identify the "before and after." That is, what was the earliest warning sign that you might have a problem, that something might go wrong? Then, what were the consequences and effects of what you thought and did? *If you can, think of something you could have done early the very same day to prevent your problem or reduce its severity.*

```
        EARLIEST WARNING SIGN THAT
        YOU MIGHT HAVE A PROBLEM

The earliest I knew I might be setting
myself for stress is when I finished
writing my report and sat back to look at
it.  At this point, I started thinking
"gosh, I wonder if this is what she
wants.  What will I do if it isn't."  I
suppose I could have done something at
this point to get ready for a
disappointment.  I could have said to
myself "Well, I'll learn from my
mistakes."
```

```
                CONSEQUENCES

This really bummed me out.  After turning
in my report I was blue and down in the
dumps for the rest of the day.
```

As you explore various stress management strategies, use your diary to describe how they worked. You can even plan ahead. Describe how you might prepare for a challenging first date or interview.

PART II
RELAXATION

If you are interested in relaxation, meditation, or mindfulness, I recommend you acquire:

Relaxation, Mediation & Mindfulness: Self-Training Manual (2005; Jonathan C. Smith, PhD).

You should also acquire either the comprehensive SARIS 7 CD package of relaxation instructions or THE RELAXATION COMPANION abbreviated 2 CD collection.

Both are available at: http://drsmith.deltalprinting.com

CHAPTER 8
HOW RELAXATION WORKS

The first defense against excessive stress is relaxation, including meditation and mindfulness. These approaches work directly on the arousal /distress part of our initial stress map formula:

STRESSORS   ➔   AROUSAL / DISTRESS

How they work is a story worth telling, one that can help you understand whys and hows of relaxation and meditation / mindfulness practice. It begins with the stress engine, the brain and body processes that contribute to stress arousal / distress.

When confronted with a threat, a tiny stress trigger in the brain, the hypothalamus, initiates hundreds of body changes that automatically awaken and energize the body for emergency action. Blood pressure and breathing increase, fuels are released into the blood stream, blood vessels expand, energizing hormones are released into the blood stream, and so on. This is the body's fight or flight stress response, the engine of arousal / distress.

This amazing process can be seen with sensitive stress laboratory equipment similar to the well-known lie detector polygraph. If you were hooked up to such a machine, sensitive detectors, about the size of small coins, would be stuck on your arms, chest, and forehead. These sensors work something like thermometers except that in addition to measuring body temperature, they measure other aspects of arousal including blood pressure, how quickly and deeply you breathe, how tense your muscles are, and so on.   These sensors are then attached to a computer that processes signal input.

Imagine after you have been hooked up, someone drops a large book on the floor with a loud bang. You feel startled and a bit nervous, in other words, a bit of arousal and distress. A series of squiggles on our computer monitor shows that the fight or flight response has been triggered. If you were asked to think about a bad day at work, we would see another jump in arousal. Thinking about a variety of stressors will cause the computer to register stress arousal. Indeed, many of the assaults of everyday living trigger bits of stress arousal so that over time we experience chronically high levels of the fight or flight response. This causes strain and distress. Health suffers. Body resistance declines. Our ability to attend productively at work, school, sports, and home is harmed.

The Relaxation Response

Psychologists and physicians have known about the fight or flight response since the start of the 20th century. However, in the early 1970's scientists made an interesting discovery. They selected individuals who learned relaxation or meditation and hooked them up to the same type of polygraph machinery we just described. Only this time, instead of inducing stress, participants were asked to practice whatever relaxation or meditation technique they had mastered.

What the researchers found revolutionized our understanding of stress. Almost immediately after they started relaxing, a constellation of changes automatically appeared, including reductions in blood pressure, breathing rate, muscle tension, levels of stress hormone, and body temperature. What the researchers had discovered was the mirror opposite of the fight or flight arousal / distress response, what physician Herbert Benson (1975) called the **relaxation response**. Just as the brain has an innate capacity to automatically trigger emergency stress arousal / distress, it has a parallel innate capacity to trigger an opposing, recuperative, and healing relaxation response. Furthermore, the relaxation response proved to be rapid and deep, more than one could achieve through just listening to music, sleep, or even hypnosis. The relaxation response is truly an important human capacity, a basic life-giving skill one acquires through a relaxation, meditation, or mindfulness technique.

How to Evoke the Relaxation Response

The relaxation response is one of the most powerful ways of cooling off the stress engine and reducing the arousal / distress part of our formula. However, doing this is no simple task. Walking the dog, listening to music, or watching TV aren't enough. One must learn and master a special set of exercises. To understand the tools available, we need to review how we can augment and maintain our levels of stress.

First, let's review the six types of self-stressing:

Stressed posture. You take on and maintain a stressful posture or body position, like crouching, bending over a computer terminal, straining your neck to read a book, holding your arms partially upright to grasp a car's steering wheel, and so on.

Stressed muscles. You tighten your grip on a steering wheel, hold your hands over a computer keyboard, lift heavy objects, strain at attention during a lecture.

Stressed breathing. You hold your breath in anticipation, deliberately subdue your breathing so as not to disturb a sleeping child (or people in a library), breathe rapidly while running away from an attacking dog. Stressed breathing is rapid, shallow, and uneven; it also involves breathing through the chest.

Stressed body focus. You focus on your body. Thoughts and fantasies stir up fight or flight responses such as queasy, sinking sensations in your gut or abdomen or a rapidly beating heart. This can make your stress worse.

Stressed emotion. You entertain negative thoughts and fantasies about a stressor. As a result you feel anxious, afraid, angry, or depressed.

Stressed attention. You strain and focus on a problem, divide your attention through multitasking, or are preoccupied with worries and concerns.

These six types of self-stressing point to six families of relaxation. To elaborate, there are hundreds of relaxation techniques. However, nearly all can be organized into six families. Each family has as an initial effect reducing a different type of self-stressing. Once this happens, techniques can have deeper effects.

Yoga stretching. You correct stressed postures and positions and in the process gently relax tense muscles.

Progressive muscle relaxation. You learn to detect when your muscles are tense, and release or let go of muscle tension.

Breathing exercises. You learn to breathe in a way that is slow, usually deep, and even. Relaxed breathing involves breathing in and out through ones abdomen, a skill called diaphragmatic breathing.

Autogenic exercises. You focus on suggestions or images targeted to relaxing self-stressed body organs or processes. Autogenic exercises are directed more towards the fight or flight response (such as a tense stomach, rapidly beating heart, or feeling flushed and warm). You imagine your abdomen feeling calm and cool, your heart beating evenly, and your heated body cooling off.

Imagery. Through imagery you entertain a fantasy of a calm and simple relaxing activity or situation that evokes positive feelings.

Meditation / Mindfulness. You learn to attend in an efficient and relaxed way and not waste energy with excessive mental strain, or dividing your attention between, worries, and concerns.

Thus, each family of relaxation develops a different skill and targets a different type of self-stressing. This is illustrated in the following chart:

Physical

Self-Stressing	Parallel Relaxation Technique
Stressed posture	Yoga stretching
Stressed muscles	Progressive muscle relaxation
Stressed breathing	Breathing relaxation techniques

Mental

Self-Stressing	Parallel Relaxation Technique
Stressed body focus	Relaxing body suggestions (Autogenic suggestion)
Stressed emotion	Relaxing imagery
Stressed attention	Meditation / Mindfulness

One important implication of this chart is that no one approach to relaxation is enough. It is best to explore and learn several approaches. Mastering relaxation and meditation / mindfulness is like creating a balanced diet. A good diet includes food from all the basic food groups, including grains, protein, fruit, healthy fats and oils, and so on. Eating just one thing, such as potato chips, isn't enough. Similarly, of each family of relaxation or meditation / mindfulness technique is like a different basic food group. Complete and balanced relaxation involves including a balance of different families of techniques.

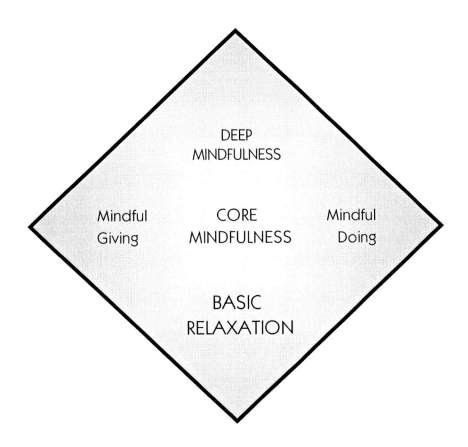

CHAPTER 9
RELAXATION AND RENEWAL

Relaxation, meditation, and mindfulness promise many rewards. The key to this promise is a basic human ability called *renewal*. *Through renewal we recover from the demands of living and return to the day fresh with energy and direction*. We "recharge our batteries," "reboot our inner computer," and "reset our personal compass" (or on-board computer navigation device). More generally, *when we experience renewal, we return to the basics of what really matters this moment*. We let go of the tensions and concerns of yesterday and tomorrow; release needless thought, judgment, and worry.

Renewal is a fundamental human capacity, one as basic as breathing and eating. Unfortunately, many people have tapped only a small part of this important ability. Let me explain. If a barking dog prevents you from completing a full night's sleep, you might wake up feeling tired and not fully ready for the day. In a small way, your renewal has been incomplete.

But renewal is more that getting a good night's sleep or taking a nap. We renew ourselves fully through silence and action, through a combination of Basic Relaxation, Mindfulness, Mindful Doing, Mindful Giving, and Deep Mindfulness. These five skills comprise what I like to call *the diamond of renewal.*

In this chapter we will explore the diamond of renewal and examine how each facet can be realized. In our journey we will be guided by a special set of road signs identified through extensive research on tens of thousands of individuals practicing dozens of diverse approaches to relaxation, meditation, and mindfulness (Smith, 2005). The road signs are called **R-States** (for "renewal states"). They will help us understand the processes of renewal, the types of renewal you might need, and when a relaxation, meditation, and mindfulness exercises may or may not be working.

Basic Relaxation

Basic relaxation involves releasing and recovering from physical and mental tension and fatigue. Our research has revealed five R-States that make up this basic type of renewal.

◆   **R-State: Sleep.** Sleep is perhaps the simplest way of letting go and getting back to basics. We let go of activity and wakefulness. Our bodies return to a recuperative vegetative state. We recover from the assaults and demands of the day and healing processes can do their work. However, sleep does more than restore our bodies. Our minds silently process the issues and problems of the day so that at times we may awaken with new solutions and insights.

Adequate sleep is a prerequisite for effective living, and meaningful relaxation, meditation, and mindfulness. If you have been without sleep for too long, your need for sleep will dominate whatever techniques you wish to practice.

◆   **R-State: Disengagement.** The first achievement of training in relaxation, meditation, and mindfulness is simply getting away (or "letting go") from the day's stressors. When we experience such Disengagement we feel distant and far away, indifferent to our cares and concerns, and nicely detached from the surrounding world. We may even lose awareness of our relaxation trainer, or of parts of our bodies.

◆   **R-State Physical Relaxation.** As you disengage, you may feel the R-State Physical Relaxation. In most general terms, you let go of unnecessary muscle tension. This can be experienced various ways. Often when our muscles are relaxed they feel nicely warm and heavy. This is a normal sign of muscle relaxation. When your body relaxes, soothing blood flows to the surface of your skin, and you may feel warm. And increased blood flow may lead to feelings of heaviness.

◆   **R-State: Mental Relaxation.** Distress comes in many forms, including frustration, pain, worry, fear, concern, or conflict. When distress is eliminated, we feel the R-State Mental Relaxation.

Mental Relaxation is associated with how we cope with problems. Imagine something is creating fear for you. Perhaps your child has gone out for the evening and is late. You feel fear. You call, and discover she is one block down the street coming home with her friends. Your mind is at ease, Mentally Relaxed. Imagine you are driving home and haven't eaten for hours. There is no place to eat in sight. Suddenly a favorite restaurant appears, and you quickly go for a delicious meal. Your hunger turns to contented satisfaction – again you are Mentally Relaxed. Maybe you are having an argument with your boss over her unfair demands. She realizes she has been pushing too hard, and agrees with your request for an easier schedule. The conflict is resolved, and you are Mentally Relaxed.

Mental Relaxation tells us something very important about the process of renewal. Resolving distressing problems is a type of action essential for experiencing all types of renewal. If you do not deal with the unfinished business of life's problems, that will limit how far you can progress with relaxation, meditation, and mindfulness.

◆   **R-State: Rested, Refreshed.** You may feel Rested and Refreshed after taking a shower, drinking a brisk cup of tea, or simply opening the window. Generally, R-State Rested and Refreshed is fleeting, mild, and experienced as short-term relief (or short-term mental-relaxation).

Core Mindfulness

Mindfulness is a term unfamiliar to many people. I like to describe it as a certain type of awareness and action, one in which we simply and fully attend to the task of the moment, undistracted by unnecessary effort or thought. Later in this program we will see that mindfulness is also a special type of meditation, one in which we train our minds to simply and calmly attend without judgement. In this chapter we consider five R-States that form everyday mindfulness.

◆   **R-State: Mindful Acceptance.** In Mindful Acceptance your mind is not cluttered with thoughts about judging what is good or bad, what you want or don't want, what you should or should not do, or how things need to be made different. The key is acceptance, recognizing the wisdom of sometimes accepting things as they are, and not struggling to change what can't be changed.

R-State Mental Relaxation, which we considered earlier, is closely linked to Mindful Acceptance. Consider the nature of acceptance. We have seen that we feel Mental Relaxation when we have truly coped with the unfinished business of what troubles us. We may experience the states of peacefulness and being at ease. If our distressing problem has been truly resolved, we can eventually accept things as they are and go on. Mindful Acceptance is both a part of mindfulness and a result of resolving sources of distress.

Mindful Acceptance is more than the relief of solving or accepting problems. It is accepting that sometimes trying to evaluate or change things just isn't necessary, a waste of time. Consider the following example of Hector, a 30-year old manager of a store that sells trendy clothing to young adults. One day, a customer enter's the store. She's wearing a ring on her nose, and has a tattoo of a spider on her wrist. Here is Hector's first reaction:

This young lady should get her act together. She is an eyesore! Kids today should be like their parents and not try so hard to be different.

Now, consider his second reaction:

Come on, Hector, get a grip. She's just a kid. And what an interesting person she seems to be. What is she trying to communicate with that tattoo? I wonder what's she's thinking in this store.

First, notice that the young lady isn't creating any problem for Hector. She's behaving politely, and may even buy some clothes. So we aren't dealing with Mental Relaxation, or the relief of resolving an issue or fixing something's that's wrong. Instead, Hector has decided that his initial reaction was simply an idle complaint, wasted hot air. Simply accepting what is, and attending to it, was much more interesting. This is an example of Mindful Acceptance.

◆　**R-State: Mindful Quiet.** Imagine you are on vacation and are sitting by yourself by a lake. Evening is approaching. The hustle and bustle of

the say has settled down. At this moment you may feel a state our research has identified as Mindful Quiet. Specifically, your feel an inner silence and calm. You aren't thinking about anything. All thought and emotional activity has settled. Your mind is quiet and still. Even feelings of peace and serenity are absent. However, you are not "numb," "zoned out," or "in a trance." This becomes more clear, like a mirror or a still lake.

◆　**R-State: Mindful Centering.** Mindful Centering goes beyond acceptance and quiet. It describes how you might experience anything in life, from what you do at work and play, your efforts at sharing, loving, and giving thanks, as well as deeper spiritual moments. When your mind is centered, it is calm, focused and undistracted. You are fully absorbed and focused on what you are doing. You are living simply in the present, not distracted by past or future concerns.

◆　**R-State: Mindful Awareness.** Mindful awareness involves feeling aware, focused, and clear.

◆　**R-State: Mindful Awakening.** Things seem fresh and new, as if you are seeing them for the first time.

Each form of mindfulness goes beyond basic relaxation. For basic relaxation, we let go of tension and get back to the basics of recovering from fatigue and tension. In mindfulness, we let go of needless thought and effort, and get back to the basics of attending to and acting in the real world, just as it is.

Mindful Doing

We can experience renewal in both the silence of relaxation, meditation, and mindfulness and in everyday activities. Our research has revealed two general types of active renewal, Mindful Doing and Mindful Giving. We focus our attention on a special set of R-States that can emerge both from the activities of doing and giving, and spontaneously from practicing relaxation, meditation, and mindfulness: Trust, Energy, Joy, Thankfulness and Love, and Prayerfulness. We begin with Mindful Doing.

◆　**R-State: Trust.** You feel trusting. You feel you can rely on someone or something, perhaps that training in relaxation, meditation, and mindfulness will work for you.

◆ **R-State: Energy.** What kinds of things do you do to get energized? What activities leave you feeling strengthened and renewed? Perhaps you have completed a challenging task, like fixing a chair or learning how to use a new computer. When done, you feel good about yourself for your achievement. You feel strengthened and confident. Such self-affirming and confidence-building acts are forms of active renewal that contribute to R-State Energy. They are mindful in that you are not distracted by irrelevant worries about deficiencies and the future.

Any type of relaxation, meditation, and mindfulness can lead to increased feelings of energy. Completing an everyday job or task that enables you to use your abilities to the full are also energizing.

◆ **R-State: Joy and Happiness.** Our research has identified a major R-State cluster most people like, one simply described as "Joy and Happiness." Think of all the types of feelings that can be described as "joyful" or "happy"? These include feeling:

Amused	Glorious	Playful
Beautiful	Harmonious	Pleased
Blessed	Hopeful	Sensuous
Childlike	Inspired	Spontaneous
Creative	Mirthful	Trusting
Delighted	Optimistic	Whole
Fun		Wonderful

Such joyful and happy feelings can spontaneously bubble up when one practices any form of relaxation, meditation, and mindfulness. They can be released when one withdraws from stress, releases tension, relaxes one's mind, and becomes more aware. They can be enjoyable products of many active pursuits (sports, leisure), and help set the stage for rewarding and meaningful practice of relaxation, meditation, and mindfulness. Joyful activities help us recover from the pressures of daily living and deepen our experience of relaxation, meditation, and mindfulness.

Mindful Giving

A second type of active renewal involves actions we do for others. We give to others mindfully when we do so fully and freely, and not because of a mechanical obligation, feelings of guilt, or desire to manipulate, or wish for payback.

◆ **R-State: Thankfulness and Love.** Occasionally practitioners of relaxation, meditation, and mindfulness report that strong and unexpected feelings of thankfulness and love emerge during their practice. A natural consequence of all R-States is a sense of gratitude and a desire to share with others, R-State Thankfulness and Love. This can be manifest as a general feeling of compassion toward others as well as feelings of forgiveness.

In everyday life it is important to remember the value of acts of thankfulness, love, compassion, and forgiveness. Not only do they help us let go of pressures that may not matter, but they nurture the practice of relaxation, meditation, and mindfulness.

◆ **R-State: Prayerful.** Relaxation, meditation, and mindfulness can stir deeply spiritual feelings. One may experience the world as awesome and mysterious, and come in touch with what is timeless, boundless, and infinite. We may express these deeper feelings in everyday life through prayerful thought and action. I use the word "prayerful" very generally as active and selfless reverence of that which is larger or greater than ourselves. Thus, to be prayerful doesn't necessarily mean saying "prayers." It is more of a deep respect we put into any type thought and action.

Let me describe this a bit differently. Silently renewed, we express our insights and understanding as to the nature of the deepest mysteries of life and that which is timeless, boundless, and infinite. We express our understanding of God, or of the godless infinite. And we act in accordance with our expressed understanding, perhaps through worship, prayer, compassion, service, or silent appreciation. Acts of prayer help us get in touch with what really matters, and enhance relaxation, meditation, and mindfulness.

Deep Mindfulness

Through Deep Mindfulness we feel renewed by going beyond basic relaxation, doing, or giving. We become deeply mindful of the immense reality that we are but a small speck in a large universe, that there things much larger and greater than ourselves. Research identifies three R-States that depict this profound letting go and getting back to bare essentials:

◆ **R-State: Deep Mystery**
◆ **R-State: Awe and Wonder**
◆ **R-State: Timeless, Boundless, Infinite, At One**

The R-States of Mystery as well as Awe and Wonder reflect a nonanalytic and goal-less awareness of a larger and greater reality that is new, awesome, beyond ordinary familiar comprehension and expectations; it is both deeply mysterious and "extra-ordinary."

Feelings of deep mystery are somewhat familiar to most people. We all have discovered things we do not understand, and sometimes we encounter profound questions and mysteries that seem to transcend any possibility of understanding.

R-State Awe and Wonder merits a bit more discussion. One might feel free and detached from the preoccupying burdens and expectations of daily life, and see the world freshly through different eyes. Awe and wonder can reflect a childlike and innocent release from adult, verbal, analytic thinking; one might feel like a small child facing a wonderful, larger world. This state can also result from momentary "decommissioning" of adult analytic thinking. The Grand Canyon can leave one "struck with awe". Here the intensity and immensity of an external stimulus leave one temporarily "shocked" or "blinded". Our language provides many phrases that convey this notion: "shock of the new," "blinding truth," "dumbstruck," "speechless," "far out," "mindblowing," "knocks one's socks off," or simply "Wow!" or "Amazing!" However expressed, one's adult, verbal, analytic thinking cap has been knocked askew; one is temporarily freed or released from these constraints and sees things anew.

At the level of deep renewal we touch upon the realm of the spiritual, of God, Higher Powers, Ultimate Concerns, or simply a principle (cosmic quantum physics) or process (evolution of consciousness) larger or greater than ourselves. It is beyond the scope of this book to specify what this deep and awesome mystery may be; the reader has both supernatural and natural options: God, Allah, the unconscious, the flow of being, the higher power, or perhaps just the night sky. Suffice it to say that atheists (those who do not accept the notion of an unprovable, supernatural/paranormal entity that answers personal prayers by altering the laws of physics and changing the course of history) can have deeply authentic spiritual experiences.

In the deepest form of silent renewal we let go of concepts. And when you let go of what you have been taught God or the universe is, you are left with the bare essentials. When you erase all the words from the blackboard, what remains is simple blackness. When you put aside all that you have

been taught about God, what remains is an awesome mystery that is utterly profound. *It* is the bare essential.

Finally, in the R-State Timeless / Boundless / Infinite one is aware of something larger or greater than oneself. But for the first time one forgets oneself as much as is absolutely possible and becomes completely aware of a transcendent "other." That is all we have to say about this state. I leave it up to you to fill in the blank.

The R-State Questionnaire

The Renewal State Questionnaire (R-State Questionnaire) is designed to help you identify the unique R-States associated with different families of relaxation. Make six copies of this questionnaire (on the following page) and complete it after you complete each new approach to relaxation.

The R-State Questionnaire (Complete right after practicing)
(PLEASE MAKE 6 COPIES, ONE FOR EACH APPROACH TO RELAXATION)

HOW MUCH DID YOU FEEL THIS DURING OR AFTER YOUR ACTIVITY?

○ **NOT AT ALL**   ① **SLIGHTLY**   ② **MODERATELY**   ③ **VERY MUCH**

BASIC RELAXATION

○ ① ② ③ **SLEEPINESS**
• I felt DROWSY and SLEEPY   • I was DOZING OFF or NAPPING

○ ① ② ③ **DISENGAGEMENT**
• I felt DISTANT and FAR AWAY.
• I felt INDIFFERENT to my cares and concerns.
• I felt nicely DETACHED from the world around me.

○ ① ② ③ **PHYSICAL RELAXATION**
• My BODY felt PHYSICALLY RELAXED.
• My muscles were SO RELAXED that they felt LIMP.
• My hands, arms, or legs were SO RELAXED that they felt WARM and HEAVY.

○ ① ② ③ **MENTAL RELAXATION**
• I felt AT EASE   • I felt PEACEFUL   • I felt CAREFREE

○ ① ② ③ **RESTED / REFRESHED**
• I felt RESTED and REFRESHED

CORE MINDFULNESS

○ ① ② ③ **MINDFUL ACCEPTANCE**
• I recognized the wisdom of sometimes ACCEPTING things as they are.
• I felt there's no need to try to change things that simply can't be changed.

○ ① ② ③ **MINDFUL QUIET**
• My mind was SILENT and calm (I wasn't thinking about anything).
• My mind was QUIET and STILL.

○ ① ② ③ **MINDFUL CENTERING**
• I felt I was living fully and SIMPLY in the PRESENT, not distracted by past or future concerns.
• I felt fully absorbed and focused on what I was doing

○ ① ② ③ **MINDFUL AWARENESS**
• I felt AWARE, FOCUSED, and CLEAR

○ ① ② ③ **MINDFUL AWAKENING**
• Things seemed FRESH and NEW, as if I were seeing them for the first time

MINDFUL DOING

○ ① ② ③ **TRUST**
• I felt TRUSTING; I could RELY on someone or something

○ ① ② ③ **ENERGIZED**
• I felt ENERGIZED and STRENGTHENED • I felt CONFIDENT

○ ① ② ③ **HAPPY**
• I was HAPPY • I was JOYFUL.

MINDFUL GIVING

○ ① ② ③ **THANKFUL AND LOVING**
• I felt THANKFUL   • I felt LOVING

○ ① ② ③ **PRAYERFUL AND REVERENT**

DEEP MINDFULNESS

○ ① ② ③ **AWE AND WONDER**
• I felt a sense of AWE and WONDER

○ ① ② ③ **DEEP MYSTERY**
• I sensed the DEEP MYSTERY of things beyond my understanding

○ ① ② ③ **TIMELESS, BOUNDLESS, INFINITE**
• Things seemed TIMELESS, BOUNDLESS, INFINITE, AT ONE

CHAPTER 10
PHYSICAL RELAXATION EXERCISES

Yogaform Stretching

Yoga originated in India over 5,000 years ago. Hundreds of schools and thousands of specific exercises have evolved. Of these, the most popular are Hatha yoga and Prana yoga. Hatha yoga focuses primarily on maintaining postures, stretching, and to some extent, breathing in a way that is relaxed. Prana yoga is primarily breathing. Yoga is associated with Eastern religion and may involve restrictions in diet and other activities. Hatha yoga can involve rigorous, difficult, and potentially dangerous positions and should be practiced under qualified professional supervision, not from a simple book or recording.

The yogaform stretching exercises in this chapter are similar to those found in Hatha yoga. However, they are very simple, easy, and not associated with any religion or philosophy. They can readily be practiced with audio or book instructions.

The idea underlying yogaform stretching is to correct stress-producing postures and positions, and to gently "stretch out" muscle tension. When tense, our muscles and joints can be likened to a tightly bent and coiled spring (or a crumpled scarf). If we wanted to straighten out and loosen the spring (or smooth out the scarf) and reduce its stiffness, we could easily stretch it out and then release the stretch. Similarly, in the yogaform exercises we slowly, smoothly, and gently stretch out each muscle, stretch our joints, and then easily release the stretch. A yoga stretch corrects stressful posture, and also reduces muscle tension and fatigue, and increases energy.

The biggest problem beginners have with yogaform stretching is that they tend to rush through the exercises, to get the effects as fast as possible. Unfortunately, yogaform stretching can't be sped up. First, it takes time to untense a muscle by stretching it out. If you stretch quickly, it simply may not work. Second, if you stretch quickly, you might trigger what is called the "stretch reflex" in which the muscles automatically tense up. Our muscles are wired in such a way that if they are

stretched too quickly, they instinctively tense up to prevent possible overstretching. So stretch very slowly, smoothly, and gently. It doesn't matter how far you stretch. You don't have to look like a master yoga practitioner tied up in knots! And it is OK if your stretching feels a little jumpy or jerky, like a rusty door that needs to be oiled. Just do the exercise as slowly, smoothly, and gently as you can. As you gain practice, your stretches will smooth out.

I recommend eleven stretching exercises, offered in *the Relaxation Companion* or *SARIS* CD series. To do them, first find a comfortable chair in which you can sit upright, with your back firmly supported and your feet flat on the floor. When you can complete the entire sequence, take the R-State Questionnaire at the end of this chapter.

Summary of Yogaform Stretching Exercises

Do each exercise twice on the right side and twice on the left (for hands, arms, legs, and feet).

Hand Stretch

Slowly, smoothly, and gently open your fingers and easily stretch them back and apart. Gently unstretch..

Arm Stretch

Slowly, smoothly, and gently slide you hand down your leg. Reach out and extend your arm in front of you. Hold the stretch, and gently return your arm.

Arm and Side Stretch

Start with both arms hanging by your sides. Slowly, smoothly and gently circle your right arm and hand up and away from your body like the hand of a clock or the wing of a bird. Reach all the way to the sky, arching your back. Then gently return your arm.

Back Stretch

Sit up straight and bow forward. Let your head fall forward, as you bow. Do not force yourself to bow over . . . let gravity pull your body toward your knees. Then, slowly straighten up.

Shoulder Stretch

Lift both arms straight ahead in front of you and let your fingers touch. Slowly, smoothly, and gently circle them around together, as if you were squeezing a big pillow. Let your hands cross, pointing in opposite directions. Squeeze farther and farther, so you can feel a stretch in your shoulders and back. Hold the stretch.. And gently release the stretch.

Back of Neck Stretch

Let your head tilt easily toward your chest, without exerting effort. Feel the stretch in the back of your neck..

Face Stretch

Slowly, smoothly, and gently open your jaws, mouth, and eyes while lifting your eyebrows, stretching the face muscles..

Front of Neck Stretch

Let your head tilt, this time backward, letting gravity do the work. Feel the front of your neck stretch.. Let gravity pull your head back

Stomach and Chest Stretch

Gently arch your stomach and chest out..Feel a stretch along your torso. Then gently and easily release the stretch.

Leg Stretch

Slowly and easily stretch the leg out in front of you. Stretch so you can feel the muscles pulling.

Foot Stretch

While resting your heel on the floor, gently pull your toes and foot up, as if they were being pulled by strings.

When finished, take the R-State Questionnaire at the end of the previous chapter. This questionnaire will help you identify the unique effects of yogaform stretching and compare stretching with other approaches. .

Progressive Muscle Relaxation

Progressive muscle relaxation is an approach to relaxation very popular among health professionals. In the late 1920's, Chicago physician, Edmund Jacobson, was looking for a way to help his anxious patients reduce their anxiety. He noted that our thoughts are often reflected in our bodies. For example, if you were to think about running away from a wild dog, your legs might actually tighten up a bit during the fantasy. While imagining the act of smiling, you might automatically smile a bit. In other words, certain thoughts lead to tension in certain muscles. Jacobson figured out a way to reverse this process. In his progressive muscle relaxation, relaxing muscles leads to a more relaxed mind. So he taught his patients the subtle skill of identifying and letting go of muscle tension.

Later, psychologists perfected this approach into what we currently call progressive muscle relaxation. The idea is simple. First, tighten up a specific muscle while the rest of the body remain relaxed. Notice how the tension feels. Then go completely limp. Let go for about 20 seconds, and attend to the feelings of relaxation. You can try this right now with your shoulders.

Attend to your shoulder muscles. While keeping the rest of your body nice and relaxed, shrug your shoulders now. Create a good shrug. Feel the sensations of shrugging. Then let go and go completely limp. Imagine your shoulders have been held up by strings (like a puppet), and the strings have been cut. Your shoulders then fall limp. Let them stay limp as you slowly count to 20. Notice what relaxation in the shoulders feels like.

People who try progressive muscle relaxation often ask why tense up a muscle in order to relax it? The idea is that tightening up first sets the stage for a relaxation rebound or "swing back" effect. Imagine a small child is sitting on a swing. To move the swing forward, you could slowly push it ahead. However, what you would probably do is pull the swing back, let go, and let the child swing forward on his own. This is the "swing back" or rebound effect similar to what happens in progressive muscle relaxation. You first tense up a muscle, let go, and let your muscles "fall" or "swing" into deeper relaxation.

Sometimes sports enthusiasts wonder why it is important to count to 20 while letting go. Why not just let go, and go right on to the next exercise, like doing isometrics. This highlights a very important point. You cannot rush the effects of progressive muscle relaxation. It takes at least 20 seconds for the muscle tension you have created to completely release. If you rush the exercise and start tensing up again before 20 seconds, your muscles haven't had time to relax, and will remain tense. At the end of the exercise, you may be more tense than you were before.

There is a second idea underlying progressive muscle relaxation. If you are reading this book indoors, there are probably many sources of potential noise you simply do not notice. Perhaps you are unaware of the constant drone of the air conditioner, heater, or outside traffic. The brain has a way of simply tuning out potential background nuisances. In a similar way, we grow numb to continuous muscle tension. We are simply less aware of how our muscles may be tightening up.

To elaborate on this idea, imagine you are watching a very long and frightening mystery movie. Your mind is completely absorbed in the scary plot. Every minute you are sitting on the edge of your seat grasping your can of cola. At the end of the movie, you sigh. Then you notice that your cola can has been crushed and that your fingers aches. You realize "Gosh, I must have been holding on real tight! I wasn't even aware of it!" For hours your hands were very very tense. However, the tension was a continuous background stimulus, which the brain has a way of automatically tuning out Psychotherapists sometimes see patients who have a lot of muscle tension. In a way, the lives of these patients are something like continuous stressful movies. If you talk with such a tense patient, he or she may well describe all the problems in their lives; but if you ask them how their muscles feel, often they will say "my muscles feel fine." Then if you look carefully, you may notice they are clenching their teeth, holding their hands tightly, and furrowing up their brow. You may see how they are actually tightening up. Yet they may be unaware that they are actually straining as much as a weight lifter! Our brain tunes out continuous feelings of muscle tension.

Nearly everyone has some tuned-out or numbed-out muscle tension. One of the major goals of progressive muscle relaxation is to teach you to detect hidden sources of tension. When you learn this skill, you have acquired a powerful new ability – you can begin to deeply let go of tension. With progressive muscle relaxation you learn to detect muscle tension, and then release it.

This chapter offers a summary of the eleven progressive muscle relaxation exercises presented in *The Relaxation Companion* or *SARIS* CD series.. First find a comfortable chair in which you can sit upright. Practice in a place free from distraction. When finished, take the R-State Questionnaire.

Progressive Muscle Relaxation Exercises

Do each exercise twice on the right side and twice on the left (for hands, arms, legs, and feet).

Hand Squeeze

Make a tight fist. If fingernails dig into your palms, you can make a fist by pressing the fingers flat against the palm, or wrapping fingers around and squeezing the thumb. Let go and go completely limp while counting to twenty.

Arm Squeeze

Touch the palm of your right hand to your right shoulder. Your arm should be bending at the elbow. Tense up your arm. Hold the tension and count to 5. Let go and go completely limp. Count to twenty while letting the muscles get more and more relaxed.

Arm and Side Squeeze

Rest your hands in your lap. Press your right arm against the side of your chest, as if squeezing a sponge in the pit of the arm. Let go and go completely limp for about 20 seconds.

Back Squeeze

Tighten the muscles in the lower back, below the shoulders. There are several ways to do this. You might pull your shoulders and elbows back, behind you. Try to touch your elbows behind your back; notice the back tensing up. You might want to imagine you are scratching an itch, rubbing your back against the back of the chair. Or push the lower back against the chair. Let go and go completely limp for about 20 seconds.

Shoulder Squeeze

Shrug the shoulders, lifting them up. Let go and go completely limp for about 20 seconds.

Back of Neck Squeeze

Gently tilt the head back, creating a slight squeeze in the muscles in the back of the neck. Let go and go completely limp for about 20 seconds.

Face Squeeze

Scrunch up the entire face, clenching the jaws, pressing the lips together, tightening up the nose and cheeks, squinting the eyes, and wrinkling the forehead. Let go and go completely limp for about 20 seconds.

Front of Neck Squeeze

Gently tilt the head forward, creating a gentle squeeze in the front of the neck. Let go and go completely limp for about 20 seconds.

Stomach and Chest Squeeze

Tighten up the stomach and chest in whatever way feels comfortable – sucking the stomach in, slightly pushing it out, or just tightening it up. Let go, go completely limp.

Leg Squeeze

Pull your right leg back pressing it against a chair leg, or just tighten it up. Feel the tension all along your leg up through the buttocks. Let go and go completely limp for about 20 seconds.

Foot Squeeze

Press your right foot into the floor. Curl your toes and press them down. Let go and go completely limp for about 20 seconds.

Breathing Exercises

Breathing reflects how relaxed or tense we are. Often you can see when someone is under stress by how they are breathing. For example, consider this fanciful description of a television show about a stressful family dinner:

Julie, the 17-year- old daughter, gleefully announces she is marrying Jody, the class delinquent, once he gets out of jail. Father gasps and holds his breath, and then while biting his lip, breathes in and out with tight control. Mother tearfully explodes, and then pleads "Haven't you thought about your future?

Your children!" Julie explains that her children (apparently at least three are on the way) can always live with Mother and Father. Mother begins to sob, her breathing very jerky and uneven. Suddenly, someone knocks on the door. Julie, gleefully screams, "It's Jody! He's out!" Father feels the anger build within. He crosses his shoulders and pumps up his chest like a prize fighter. You can see his shoulders rise, as if he were carrying the entire world on his back. Now, he's breathing rapidly.

I leave it to you to imagine how this plot unfolds. However, notice one subplot, the story of how Mother and Father are breathing. We see all the signs of stressed breathing. They are:

1. Rapid breathing
2. Uneven breathing
3. Shallow breathing (usually, but not always)
4. Breathing using the chest and shoulders.

Relaxed breathing is just the opposite. Imagine a sleeping baby, at rest in complete calm and comfort. Her breathing is:

1 Slow and easy
2. Very easy and even
3. Nice and deep
4. Diaphragmatic (abdominal)

The first three characteristics of relaxed breathing are not difficult to see. But what is diaphragmatic breathing? Relaxed breathing feels like you are breathing in and out through your stomach or abdomen. Of course, this is not what really happens. Relaxed breathing feels like abdominal breathing because of a special muscle, the diaphragm.

Think of where your stomach is. Now think of where your lungs are. Separating your lungs and your stomach is thin, flat wall, a muscle called the diaphragm. When the diaphragm moves down, guess what happens. Because it is moving down, air is drawn into your lungs, and your stomach is pushed out. And when your diaphragm moves up towards your lungs, you exhale and your stomach is pulled in.

Another way of thinking of this is to think of a piston moving up and down. When it moves down, it pulls air in. When it moves up, it pushes air out. The stomach, of course, has no where to go, so when the diaphragm moves down it pushes the stomach out, and when it moves up, it pulls the stomach in.

When we are under stress, we are more likely to pump up our chests like boxers or angry chest-pounding gorillas. Our ribcage opens up and our shoulder muscles lift, pulling air in. This is called chest breathing, and not only is it associated with stress, but it isn't a good way of breathing. The reason is somewhat technical. When you breathe diaphragmatically, you pull air all the way down your lungs, so more oxygen gets in your blood. When you chest breathe, you pull air only partway down, so less oxygen gets in your blood. To make up for this, you have to chest breathe more quickly and with greater effort. When you breathe diaphragmatically, you get more oxygen in your blood with less effort. Diaphragmatic breathing is slower and easier.

This book summarizes three sets of exercises designed to foster relaxed breathing. See *The Relaxation Companion* or *SARIS* CD set for complete instructions. The first are relatively active and involve stretching while breathing. The stretches actually help you to slow down and use your diaphragm more. Slowly walk through each exercise until you are sure you can do the moves in a slow, smooth, and comfortable manner.

Because we offer three sets of breathing exercises, you may want to take the R-States Questionnaire after each. Or if you do the entire sequence, just take one. When finished, take the R-State Questionnaire.

Breathing and Stretching Exercises

Slight Bowing and Breathing

Let your arms hang by your sides. Gently exhale as you bow forward a few inches. And then gently inhale as you slowly sit up. Make your movements smooth and effortless.

Leaning Breathing

Let your arms hang by your sides. Then lean back while taking in a slow, full breath, and then slowly sit up while breathing out. Let the air flow very smoothly and gently.

Bowing Breathing

Bow all the way forward while breathing out. Bend at your waist, letting gravity pull your torso closer and closer to your knees. And when you are ready breathe in, sit up.

Breathing Stretches

As you breathe in, slowly lift and circle your arms in front of you, and reach higher to the sky. And lower your arms to your sides as you breathe out.

Slow Bowing Breathing

In this exercise take three breaths while bowing forward. And three breaths while sitting up. Here's how. First let your arms hang by your sides. Take a deep breath. Count to keep pace. Think "one" and very slowly and smoothly begin to bow forward, just a few inches, until you have exhaled. When ready, pause and inhale. Stay in your position. Think "Two" and resume bowing over a bit farther while letting the air flow out. When you have exhaled, just pause and gently inhale. And think "Three." Continue bending over, all the way, letting gravity pull you down as you breathe out. When ready pause, and breathe naturally if you need to. You are now bowing completely over and are ready to begin to sit up. First, gently take a breath and exhale. Think "one" and begin to sit up very slowly while breathing in. When your lungs are full, pause. Think "two" exhale, and continue sitting up while breathing in. And again, pause, exhale, think "three," inhale while sitting up.

Diaphragmatic Breathing Exercises

Our second set of exercises target diaphragmatic breathing. Many people have special difficulty learning to breathe diaphragmatically and need the assistance of a trainer. Try these exercises. If you still have trouble breathing diaphragmatically, and do not have a trainer, that's OK. Just go on to the next exercise.

Stomach Squeeze Breathing

Sit up in your chair and open your hands and fingers and place them over your stomach. Spread your fingers comfortably apart so they cover your entire stomach, with your thumbs touch the bottom part of your chest. Gently press your fingers into your stomach as you breathe out, and release your fingers as you breathe in. See if you can feel the movement of your stomach, filling and emptying with air.

Stomach Touch Breathing

Sit up in your chair with your hands and fingers placed over your stomach. Let your hands and fingers remain relaxed. Do not press in. Gently breathe in, as if you were filling your stomach with air, and exhale, so you can feel the rise and fall of your stomach. Continue breathing this way, slowly and easily. Notice air filling and emptying your stomach.

Book Breathing

You might want to practicing this exercise while lying on your back on the floor. And you need a book. Gently place a book over your abdomen. Adjust your book so it does not fall off. Let yourself breathe easily and naturally. Breathe so you can notice the movement of the book on your abdomen. Adjust your book so you can see its movement more clearly. The up and down movement of your book shows if you are breathing using your abdomen.

Passive Breathing Exercises

The following breathing exercises are somewhat different from the one's we have tried. They are very passive and involve very little movement. These exercises are excellent for fostering breathing that is slow, smooth, and even.

Sniffing

Rest your hands comfortably in your lap. Let yourself relax. As you breathe in, imagine you are sniffing a very delicate flower. Breathe in slowly with many gentle little sniffs. Let the flow of breath into your nose be as smooth and gentle as possible, so you barely rustle a petal. Take a full breath.. And when ready, relax, letting yourself breathe out slowly and naturally, without sniffing.

Blowing and Breathing

Take a slow deep breath and pause. Breathe out slowly though your lips, as if you were blowing at a candle flame just enough to make it flicker, but not go out. Breathe in through your nose.

Occasional Deep Breaths

Let yourself breathe easily and naturally. Take in a full deep breath, filling your lungs and abdomen with good, refreshing air. And when you are ready, relax. And slowly let the air flow out, very smoothly and gently. And now, just continue breathing normally for a while, without taking in deep breaths. And, again, when you are ready, take in another full deep breath, filling your lungs, with good, energizing air. Repeat three times, following every three normal breaths with a deep breath.

Focused Breathing

Simply breath in a relaxed manner, in and out through your nose. Become fully aware of the air as it rushes in and out, flowing into and out of your lungs filling your body with refreshing and renewing air. Calmly focus on the unhurried rhythm of your breathing. Let yourself breathe effortlessly, without strain.

CHAPTER 11
MENTAL RELAXATION EXERCISES

Autogenic Training

Can you simply think your body into relaxation? At first, this may seem like a type of wishful thinking. However, since 1900, relaxation therapists have the powers of the mind to evoke physical relaxation.

We experience the powers of the mind and the body every day. Imagine you are preparing for a wonderful meal. You think about the delicious food and how it might smell. You can almost taste the juicy flavors. If you spend the next 60 seconds fantasizing about your favorite food, chances are you will start salivating – a physiological response! Simple thoughts have the capacity to evoke a physiological reaction.

Now think about a stressful encounter. Imagine a recent confrontation that made you a bit angry. Think about everything that happened, what they did and said, what you said and did, what was unfair, and so on. Quite likely you might feel some physical changes as your blood begins to "boil," and perhaps your stomach tighten up. Or picture the most frightening thing that ever happened to you. Replay this fantasy in your mind, including every detail. Does your stomach begin to feel queasy? Does your heart begin to beat more quickly? These fantasies illustrate the power of the mind to stir body reactions.

At the onset of the 20th century, neorophysiologist Oskar Vogt was studying the effect of hypnosis on his patients. He noticed that when his patients began to relax, they often reported certain physical sensations, such as feeling warm and heavy, a slowly beating heart, and a comforting warmth in the abdominal area. Later psychiatrist Johannes Shultz took this idea and developed an approach to relaxation that simply reversed this process. Patients were instructed to passively repeat suggestions of warmth, heaviness, a slowly beating heart, and comforting warmth in the abdomen. He found that suggestions of physical relaxation could evoke physical relaxation. This idea became the core autogenic training, as presented in this book, autogenic suggestion.

The instructions for autogenic suggestion re very simple. Find a quiet relaxing place to settle down. Close your eyes. And then let any of the following sets of words and related images float through your mind:

> *"Hands and arms warm and heavy."*
> *"Hand and arms in the warm sun (or sand or water).*
>
> *"Heart beating calm and easy.*
> *"Heart beating like a lazy clock."*
>
> *"Abdomen warm and soothed."*
> *"Abdomen warm and soothed, like after drinking soup or hot chocolate, or sitting in the sun."*

However, there is a trick in doing this to make it work. It is important not to exert any effort when repeating your words or pictures. Do not actively try to obtain the result you suggest. In fact, be completely indifferent as to whether or not the suggestions actually work. Let the words or pictures simply float lazily through your mind, like meaningless echoes.

It is easy to see why it is important to take this stance of easy indifference. Let's try this experiment. First, rest your hands on a table or your lap. Now, for the next minute or so, try to deliberately and effortfully create feelings of warmth and heaviness in your hands and arms.

> *Try to make your hands and arms warm and heavy. Work really hard at it. Concentrate! Order your hands and arms to feel warm and heavy. In your mind, speak with considerable force and effort. Now continue with this for a minute.*

> *Now, let go and try something completely different. It doesn't matter a bit if your arms and hands actually get warm and heavy. Not a bit. Simply imagine some meaningless words and pictures slowly floating through your mind, "hands and arms*

warm and heavy . . . hands and arms warm and heavy . . . hands and arms warm and heavy." Let these phrases slowly go over and over and over. Continue for the next minute or so.

I find that about 80 percent of those who try this exercise actually feel their hands and arms grown warm and heavy when they let go and passively let phrases and images float through their mind. And that is the secret to autogenic suggestion. Don't try. Don't exert effort. Let words and images float through your mind easily and lazily.

What happens with autogenic suggestion? Each suggestion seems to target a slightly different aspect of physical stress. For example, when aroused with stress, less blood flows to our extremities, our hands, arms, legs, and feet, so they feel cold and clammy. So thinking warmth, counters this part of the stress response.

What about feelings of heaviness? Have you ever been so relaxed that your body felt heavy, and you just couldn't get yourself to move out of bed? If you think about it, each part of the body weighs something. A hand weighs as much as, perhaps, a baseball. When we're tense, we rarely notice this weight. When we are relaxed, and less distracted by other sensations, we are more likely to notice sensations that remain, including the sensation of the heaviness of our hands, arms, legs, and feet. When deeply relaxed, we feel heavy. Thinking suggestions of heaviness reverses the process and helps relax the muscles.

The heart obviously beats harder and faster when under stress. Autogenic suggestions of a calmly and easily beating heart counter this.

And, when feeling a stressful emotion, nerves deep in our abdomen, our "gut brain," evoke certain stress sensations, such as queasiness, butterflies, and even upset. Autogenic suggestions of feeling comforting warmth in the abdomen counter this.

By targeting these types of self-stressing, autogenic suggestions not only help us relax specific parts of the body, but eventually they lead to overall relaxation.

The following autogenic suggestions are not to be used as a precise formula or chant. Instead, they are gentle suggestions of what types of thoughts or images to let float through your mind. Simply read over one category of suggestion, then close your eyes, lean back, and for about five minutes let suggestions like these float through your mind. Whenever your mind wanders, that's fine. Gently return to letting your autogenic suggestions float through your mind. Spend from 2 - 5 minutes with

each category of suggestion. I recommend listening to the instructions presented in *The Relaxation Companion* or *SARIS* CD series. When finished, take the R-State Questionnaire.

Once you have mastered the idea of autogenic suggestion, try suggestions targeted to specific parts of the body other than the limbs, heart, or abdomen. If you feel the beginnings of a headache, you may want to think "head and neck, cool and relaxed." For stomach distress, "stomach soothed and calm." If you are getting a tooth filled at a dentist, you might think of pain sensations as "cool, like an ice cube." There are two general principles when inventing new autogenic suggestions:

1. Be sure you have identified a specific body part that feels uncomfortable. Therefore, do not pick "My body feels unwell" or "I feel sick."
2. Invent a suggestion that identifies a sensation or image that is either the opposite of the target discomfort ("my burning stomach feels cool") or transforms the uncomfortable sensation into a sensation that may well be similar, but not as uncomfortable. That is, instead of focusing on all the negative associations of a stomach ache, think how the ache can be made into a positive fantasy ("My stomach burns as healing blood rushes to it, burning off toxins." This is a popular strategy for managing pain. ("The sensation of a dentist drilling . . . cool water flowing on my tooth.")

Autogenic Suggestions

Warmth and Heaviness

Hands and arms, warm and heavy. Like resting in the sun. Like feeling warm water. Like magnets are pulling them down. Tension dissolves and flows away. You feel distant and far away. Indifferent.
Repeat for legs and feet.

Calmly Beating Heart

Heart is beating calm and even. Soft and easy, calm and easy. Tension dissolves and flows away.

Abdomen

Attend to an area above your abdomen. Warm and soothed. Comfortable and warm. Like feeling warm and good after drinking warm hot chocolate, or good soup

Imagery

Imagery is an exercise nearly everyone knows how to do. You simply entertain a special type of fantasy. However, there is a difference between imagery as relaxation and everyday fantasy. Everyday fantasies can involve considerable activity. You might think about winning a game, arguing, having sex, and so on. In relaxation imagery we do none of this. The point is to select a pleasant imagery theme that involves as little effort or activity as possible.

The relaxation theme you pick can be a fantasy of a past situation or activity, or something completely imaginary. We have found four categories of imagery to especially popular: travel, outdoor/nature, water, and indoor. You can find examples of each on the next page.

Four Types of Imagery Themes

Travel

Airplane, bird, blimp, bus, car, cruise ship, horse-drawn carriage, floating in air, floating dandelion seed, flying saucer, flying like a bird, hot-air balloon, jet, kite, magic cow, motorcycle, ocean liner, raft, parachute, rocket into space, ship, roller blades, skateboard, submarine, train, wagon, walking.

Outdoor/Nature

Church retreat, campgrounds, clouds, desert, forest, garden, island, meadow, monastery, mountain, nature preserve, nudist camp, outer space, park, planet (mars,etc.) spa, valley, storybook land, zoo

Water

Beach, brook, creek, glacier, hot tub, lake, ocean, pond, rain, rain forest, mist, river, sauna, ski slopes, shower, snow, steam bath, stream, swimming pool, wading pond, waterfall

Indoor

Cabin, castle, cave, cavern, childhood house, church, dream house, meditation room, mosque, palace, prayer room, skyscraper, school room, secret hiding place, synagogue, tavern, temple, tree house, vacation home

---

There is another important difference between everyday fantasy and relaxation imagery. Fantasy is often spontaneous and unplanned. Relaxation imagery calls for some initial preparation. Specifically:

1. Select your imagery topic;
2. Think of sense details, what you see, hear, feel on your skin, and smell;

3. Check for problems, and revise your imagery.

Once you have done the necessary preparation, simply enjoy your imagery for 10 to 20 minutes. I recommend the instructions in *The Relaxation Companion* or *SARIS* CD series.

Relaxation Imagery

Selecting your Imagery Topic

What type of image appeals to you most? From the list in the box on the previous page, pick your category of imagery:

My Preferred Type of Imagery

Now, select a specific topic. For example, if you picked "Outdoor /Nature," name the setting:

My Specific Imagery Topic

Fill in the Sense Details

You are ready to fill in the sense details. Let your mind wander. Have some fun. Think freely. There is no reason to come up with a "correct" or "complete" list. Just think of a handful of details for each of the following sense modalities:

What do you see? (List about five things)

What do you hear? (About 5 things)

```
+---------------------------------+
| What to you feel touching your  |
|          skin?                  |
|       (About 3 things)          |
|                                 |
|                                 |
|                                 |
|                                 |
|                                 |
+---------------------------------+
```

```
+---------------------------------+
| What fragrances do you smell?   |
|          (2 or 3)               |
|                                 |
|                                 |
|                                 |
|                                 |
|                                 |
+---------------------------------+
```

```
+--------------------------------------------+
|   What do you hear?  (About 5 things)      |
|                                            |
| I hear the gentle stepping of my horse.    |
| I hear my horse breathing easily.          |
| I hear the wind passing by my ears.        |
| I hear birds in the air.                   |
| I hear the breeze brushing through the     |
| trees.                                     |
|--------------------------------------------|
| What to you feel touching your skin?       |
|           (About 3 things)                 |
|                                            |
| I feel the pressure of my horse supporting |
| my body.                                   |
| I feel the wind on my skin.                |
| I feel the soothing sun.                   |
|--------------------------------------------|
| What fragrances do you smell?  (2 or 3)    |
|                                            |
| I smell the fresh grass.                   |
| I smell the pleasant aroma of leather      |
+--------------------------------------------+
```

Any Possible Problems or "Booby Traps"?

You are just about ready to begin your imagery exercise. However, just to be careful, review what you have selected. Sometimes people select an imagery topic that stirs up an unexpected negative association. For example, perhaps you selected "resting on the ocean beach" as your peaceful image, only to realize during the image that you once were seriously sunburned on the beach. It would be better to adjust this imagery by inserting a shade tree. Do you foresee any such booby traps in your image?

Examples

```
+----------------------------------+
|  My Preferred Type of Imagery    |
|                                  |
|           TRAVEL                 |
|----------------------------------|
|   My Specific Imagery Topic      |
|                                  |
| RIDING HORSEBACK THROUGH THE WOODS|
|----------------------------------|
| What do you see? (List about five things)|
|                                  |
| I am riding my very trusted old friend, |
| Duke.                            |
| I see the soft brown hair on his head and|
| his ears flopping.              |
| The fields of peaceful green grass pass |
| by.                              |
| From time to time we pass under a huge, |
| arching tree.                   |
| The sky is pure blue, without a cloud.  |
| I see birds overhead.           |
+----------------------------------+
```

```
+--------------------------------------------+
|   My Preferred Type of Imagery             |
|                                            |
|             WATER                          |
|--------------------------------------------|
|   My Specific Imagery Topic                |
|                                            |
| RESTING NEXT TO A GENTLE WATERFALL         |
|--------------------------------------------|
| What do you see?  (List about five things) |
|                                            |
| I see the water flowing down rocks above.  |
| I see the waterfall splashing into a pond. |
| I see the rippling pond next to me.        |
| I see patches of flowers next to the pond. |
| I see a few tiny goldfish in the pond.     |
|--------------------------------------------|
| What do you hear?  (About 5 things)        |
|                                            |
| I hear the gentle gurgle of water flowing. |
| I hear the water flowing under my feet.    |
| I hear the soft spray of water as it       |
| touches the surrounding ground.            |
| I hear an occasional fish splash.          |
| I hear my feet as they dangle in the pond. |
| I hear the breeze brushing through the     |
| trees.                                     |
|--------------------------------------------|
| What to you feel touching your skin?       |
|           (About 3 things)                 |
|                                            |
| I feel spray of water on my face.          |
| I feel the cool air evaporating the water. |
| I feel the warm sun.                       |
|--------------------------------------------|
| What fragrances do you smell?  (2 or 3)    |
|                                            |
| I smell the clean scent of water.          |
| I smell the flowers.                       |
+--------------------------------------------+
```

When finished, with your imagery exercise take the R-State Questionnaire.

Concentrative Meditations

Meditation is a very simple exercise. In fact, the instructions can be said in two sentences: Calmly attend to a simple stimulus. Calmly return your attention after every distraction . . . again and again and again.

Most schools of meditation teach one technique. Two very popular approaches are Zen and transcendental meditation (tm). In Zen one attends to the flow of breath or attending to the present moment; tm teaches a simple meditation syllable or mantra

However, researchers at Chicago's Roosevelt University Stress Institute have found that different forms of meditation work for different people, and no one approach works for everyone. The best way to find your meditation is to try the many approaches that have evolved over the years. This chapter presents instructions for seven approaches called concentrative meditation. They all involve calmly restricting attention to a simple stimulus.

This is were most beginning meditators get confused. To work, a meditation target stimulus has to be **really simple**, with no details that might distract or evoke thoughts, feelings, memories, and so on. It should be as **utterly simple as possible**. Meditating on a statue of a religious icon is to complex. Too many associations. Meditating on a river is too complex. Too many details.

Meditating on what's outside the window definitely won't work. There's just too much to look at. Think of some very very simple stimuli, like:

A candle flame
The flow of your breath
A doorknob (yes, this has been used!)
The sound "hummm.

I have organized the many target stimuli people use for meditation into three groups. **Meditations of the body** focus on physical sensations. **Meditations of the mind** focus on thoughts and images. And **meditations of the senses** focus on what you see and hear.

The most common difficulty people have with meditation, and the most import part of meditation instructions, is dealing with distraction. Everyone experiences distracting thoughts and feelings when trying to meditate. This is true for both beginning and advanced meditators. You may want to meditate on a simple candle flame. At first, your mind may quietly settle into the exercise as you peacefully dwell on the flame. Then you think: "I need to make a phone call. I forgot to call my husband." Catching yourself, you return to attending to the flame. All goes well, until you begin thinking "When will this exercise be over? Is it time yet?" You catch yourself and return.

Calmly sustaining focus on a single stimulus may seem simple, but it is difficult, especially when you do it without strain or effort. The object is not to forcefully concentrate, as if you were playing a video game (where a lapse of attention might cost you millions of points). The idea is to keep your mind on your target without any effort or strain. You can't make or force yourself to do that because . . . making or forcing yourself is a type of effort or strain!

So how do you learn to meditate? Practice, practice, and practice. Actually, distraction is what makes meditation work. You simply cannot develop your meditative skills without distraction. It's like lifting weights to build muscles. You can't force your muscles to grow all at once. It takes time. You lift every day, again and agin and again. Similarly, with meditation, you return your mind from every distraction, back to your target stimulus, again and again and again. And you do so very easily, without getting flustered or upset. It's as if you are doing a very important task and get a distracting phone call. You do not get upset over the call; the person making the call didn't know you were busy. You simply and politely say, "Gosh, I'm sorry, but I can't talk with you right now. I'm involved with something. May I call you back?" And you easily return to your task.

One good way to help with distraction is to precede meditation with 15 or 20 minutes of a relaxation exercise that works well for you.
Traditionally, meditation is combined with yoga or breathing exercises. I recommend trying several of the six families, and picking what works best. These are in *The Relaxation Companion* or *SARIS* CD series. When finished, take the R-State Questionnaire.

Meditations of the Body

Body sense meditation. Attend to how the body feels when it begins to relax. Does it feel warm? Sinking? Heavy? Perhaps you notice a warm glow in your abdomen, like the good feeling from drinking hot chocolate or soup. For the next minute or so, simply let go of tension, and quietly attend to how your body feels. Whenever you start thinking about what you are doing, simply let go of these thoughts, and return to attending to how your body feels.

Rocking meditation. Let yourself begin to rock back and forth in your chair. Let each movement become more and more gentle and easy. Let yourself rock effortlessly. Let your body move on its own, in its own way, at its own speed. All you have to do is simply attend. Let each movement become more and more subtle so that someone watching would barely notice you are rocking. For the next minute or so, quietly attend to gentle and silent rocking.

Breathing meditation. Take in a full breath, and relax. Let your breathing continue on its own in a way that is free and easy. There is nothing you have to so. Simply attend to the flow of breath, in and out. And return your attention whenever your mind wanders or is distracted. Close your eyes and try this for a minute.

Meditations of the Mind

Mantra meditation. Let a relaxing word, perhaps the word peace, come to you like an echo in the distance. Let the word go over and over and over, at its own pace and volume. Close your eyes and try this for a minute.

Meditation on a visual image. With your eyes closed, think of the image of a simple spot of light, a candle flame, or a star. Calmly attend. Calmly return after every distraction. Close your eyes and try this for a minute.

Meditations of the Senses

Meditation on an external image. Slowly open your eyes halfway. Easily gaze on the candle in front of you. Whenever your mind wanders, gently return.

Meditation on sounds. Quietly listen to the sounds that you hear, without dwelling on any particular sound. Close your eyes and try this.

Mindfulness Meditation

Mindfulness is a relaxation technique, a type of meditation, and a way of approaching all of life, including stress. It is an approach that is difficult to describe. At one level, the instructions are simple:

Attend to every stimulus that comes to mind. Do so without deliberate thought or judgement. Just attend. Whenever you find yourself getting caught up in thinking about what you are attending to, return to attending.

Mindfulness as Relaxation

When done as a relaxation technique, one simply puts aside all thought, and simply notes whatever sound, sight, smell, feeling, or body sensation that comes to mind. In everyday life we occasionally enjoy this type of mindful relaxation:

You are spending a relaxing evening at a campsite, resting on the grass, simply watching the stars. You are on vacation and have put all of the cares and concerns of the day aside. Your mind is at peace, as you easily gaze above. Unexpectedly, you notice a breeze. It caresses your skin-, and settles into silence. You simply gaze overhead. In the distance a bird sings its song, and becomes still. Your mind is quiet, without thought. You see a silver cloud, reflecting the moon floating overhead. Then is quietly evaporates into complete silence.

Or you might be sitting by a slowly moving stream watching what floats by:

It is a peaceful, lazy day. You are comfortably sitting on a rock with your feet dangling in the stream. You gaze easily at the coming and going of the river. A green leaf floats into sight. You note it, and it floats away. Then you notice a shiny single bubble as it floats into sight. Very gently it pops and disappears into silence. You sit silently and attend to the flow of the river. Deep in the waters you see a goldfish and it swims away. Again, complete silence.

Mindfulness meditation is different from concentrative meditation in one important way. With concentrative meditation, you select a target stimulus, such as a mantra or candle flame. With mindfulness meditation, you do not pick a target stimulus. You simply and calmly attend to the coming and going of whatever comes to mind.

Mindfulness meditation has one important similarity to concentrative meditation. In both you can be distracted. If you are attending to everything in mindfulness, what are the distractions? In mindfulness, any **unnecessary thought** is a distraction. When mindfully attending to, say, the night sky, you might find yourself analyzing what you are viewing. You might try to identify certain stars, figure out which are actually planets, and so on. This is a distracting thought, utterly unnecessary to the "task" of attending to the night sky. One puts it aside and continues attending.

Or you might find yourself judging and evaluating what you are experiencing. You might think "I like this, it feels so comfortable. There are not enough stars, the sky is too cloudy. I want this to last forever." These judgments and evaluations are thoughts, to be gently put aside as one continues to simply attend.

And you might find yourself thinking about something completely different. You might begin reviewing the problems of the week, your obligations and so on. Again, such thoughts are unnecessary. Gently put them aside.

As with concentrative meditation, one puts thoughts aside very easily, without making a big fuss. One does so again and again and.

Mindfulness as Stress Management

Mindfulness can be more than a type of relaxation. It can be a way of approaching all of the tasks and challenges of life. It can be a type of stress management. Here, one simply attends to what can and needs to be done this moment, and gently puts aside unnecessary thought. Worry and preoccupation are viewed as distractions. Do not exert effort to exclude them or push them aside. Simply accept them (like random sounds in the night) and go on with what you are doing.

Every exercise in this book can be done mindfully. Simply focus on the task of the exercise; extraneous thought, worry, and judgment are distractions. Some pieces of simple advice are actually suggestions to be mindful: "One step at a time," "Attend to the present," "Haste makes waste" or simply "Just do it."

Some of the exercises in this book are good ways of reducing distractions to mindfulness. Consider all the techniques related to worry and distorted, unrealistic thinking. Others, such as problem-solving and brainstorming, are ways of engaging in simple and focused mindful activity.

Our approach to mindfulness is called graduated mindfulness. It involves starting with relatively simple instructions to mindfully attend to various sensations, and then progresses to mindfully attending to everything. I recommend the instructions in *The Relaxation Companion* or *SARIS* CD series.

Being Mindful of Taste

Image a wonderful bowl of pieces of your favorite fruit. And now identify your favorite piece. Imagine you have taken a piece of fruit you especially like and have placed it in your mouth. Feel its cool shape and texture. Slowly bite down. You feel the fruit squeezing as it is crushed and releases its juices in your mouth. You can smell its fresh sweet scent. You can sense the cool liquid flowing in your mouth. The fresh fruit flavor spreads over your tongue.

It's cool and delicious. As you move your tongue, the flavor dissolves. As you swallow, the juice flows away, leaving a wonderful taste in your mouth. This was a taste of mindfulness. You simply attended to a sensation. Without thought. Without analysis. Without effort.

Being Mindful of Breathing

Easily take in a full, deep breath, filling your lungs and abdomen with air. And when you are ready, simply exhale. Breathe naturally. Notice the air as it touches and flows into your nose. Notice the gentle rush of air as it flows in. Simply attend to the air, as it flows in and out of your nose. There is no need to control your breathing in any way. Whenever your mind wanders, or you start thinking about what you are doing, simply let go of your thoughts. Just attend to the flow of air. Attend to the path the air takes as it moves deeper into your nose and throat. Attend to the flow of air as it fills your lungs.

Being Mindful of the Body

Attend to how your body feels. Can you feel your feet touching the floors? The pressure of your shoes or socks on your feet? Can you feel your legs and thighs against the chair as you sit firmly and comfortably? Can you feel you back against the back of your chair? Simply attend to your body, and notice whatever sensations come and go. Whenever you notice a sensation, gently note it, let go, and continue attending. Whenever you find yourself thinking about what you like or dislike, figuring things out, or are distracted in any way, gently let go of the though or distraction, and attend to your body.

Being Mindful of Thoughts

Attend to your mind, as thoughts come and go. There is no reason to try to do or think anything. No need to try to keep thoughts away. No need to pursue or figure thoughts out. No need to hold onto a thought. Simply wait and attend. Whenever a thought or feeling comes to mind, just note it, let go, and continue attending.

Being Mindful of Sounds

Attend to the sounds you hear. Without selecting any particular sound, let sounds come to you. When you notice a particular sound, do not dwell or cling. Do not think about it. Just gently note it, let go, and continue waiting. Sounds come and go, like the wind at night or the songs of birds. Simply attend.

Full Mindfulness

Gently open your eyes and be mindful of the world of the moment. There is nothing to do, think about, or figure out. You are simply a mirror, reflecting the river of time as it flows by, minute by minute. Quietly attend and wait. When you notice something, a sight, sound, thought, or sensation, let go. And resume attending. Doing nothing. Waiting for what comes to you. You are the neutral observer, thinking nothing, doing nothing to interfere. For the next few minutes, continue being mindful of the world around you.

CHAPTER 12
MAKING YOUR OWN
RELAXATION RECORDING

The most powerful way of learning relaxation techniques is to combine exercises from the six families of approaches into a personalized program. You can then make a tape of the exercises that work best and practice with the tape.

Recall that there are six basic families of relaxation techniques:

1. Yoga stretching
2. Progressive muscle relaxation
3. Breathing exercises
4. Autogenic suggestion
5. Imagery
6. Meditation /mindfulness

In my opinion, each approach has a different effect. Each is good for something different. Learning one technique alone is incomplete; I believe you need to combine exercises from many approaches.

I think of relaxation as something like a meal. A completely balanced and nutritious meal contains foods from each of the major food groups – some protein, vegetables, fruits, carbohydrates, and so on. The same is true with relaxation. A complete "nutritious" relaxation sequence contains a variety of exercises from each relaxation "food group," – yoga stretching, progressive muscle relaxation, breathing, autogenic suggestion, imagery, and meditation and mindfulness.

In this chapter you will learn how to select and combine exercises into a personalized program, and how to make a recording of your individualized sequence. There are some important advantages to this type of individualized program:

- You select those exercises you need most
- You combine exercises in a way that is interesting and meaningful
- Because the exercise sequence is yours, you are more likely to practice.

We now walk through the steps of making your own relaxation program. Copying exercise instructions from the relaxation chapters in this book, and then add details.

Step 1: Learn All 6 Families to Relaxation

In order for this system to work, you first must learn and try all six approaches to relaxation taught in this book. It is recommend you use the *Relaxation Companion* or *SARIS* CD series.

Step 2: Select Specific Exercises you Like

Now go back over what you have learned. What approaches worked best? Progressive muscle relaxation? Imagery? Meditation? Look at your Relaxation Questionnaires. Then select specific exercises for each approach on this menu.

YOGAFORM STRETCHING

❏ HAND STRETCH
❏ ARM STRETCH
❏ ARM AND SIDE STRETCH
❏ BACK STRETCH
❏ SHOULDER STRETCH
❏ BACK OF NECK STRETCH
❏ FACE STRETCH
❏ FRONT OF NECK STRETCH
❏ STOMACH AND CHEST STRETCH
❏ LEG STRETCH
❏ FOOT STRETCH

PROGRESSIVE MUSCLE RELAXATION (If you want some exercises from this group, I recommend selecting at least 6 in order to get a complete effect)

❏ HANDS
❏ ARMS
❏ ARMS AND SIDES
❏ BACK
❏ SHOULDERS
❏ BACK OF NECK
❏ FACE
❏ FRONT OF NECK
❏ STOMACH AND CHEST
❏ LEGS
❏ FEET

BREATHING

❏ SLIGHT BOWING AND BREATHING
❏ LEANING BREATHING
❏ BOWING BREATHING
❏ STRETCHING BREATHING
❏ SLOW BOWING BREATHING
❏ STOMACH SQUEEZE BREATHING
❏ STOMACH TOUCH BREATHING
❏ BOOK BREATHING
❏ SNIFFING
❏ BLOWING
❏ OCCASIONAL DEEP BREATHS
❏ FOCUSED BREATHING

AUTOGENIC TRAINING

❏ HANDS AND ARMS VERY HEAVY
❏ HANDS AND ARMS VERY WARM
❏ ABDOMEN WARM AND SOOTHED
❏ EVENLY BEATING HEART

IMAGERY

❏ DETAILS

    Your imagery theme

    What you see:

    What you hear

    What you feel touching your skin

    What you smell

MEDITATION / MINDFULNESS

❏ BODY SENSE MEDITATION
❏ ROCKING MEDITATION
❏ MEDITATION ON BREATH
❏ MANTRA MEDITATION (NAME YOUR MANTRA)
❏ MEDITATION WITH EYES CLOSED ON VISUAL IMAGE
    (NAME YOUR VISUAL IMAGE)
❏ MEDITATION ON A SOUND (PICK SOUND)
❏ MEDITATION ON SOMETHING YOU SEE
    (NAME WHAT YOU W ILL BE LOOKING AT)
❏ MINDFULNESS MEDITATION

Step 3: Arrange your Exercises

Now, go back to your selection and decide the order in which you wish to practice.

• Put physical exercises, like PMR, yoga stretching, and stretching breathing, at the beginning.
• Put meditation and imagery near the end.
• Blend passive breathing exercises (examples: breathing out through your lips; deep breathing) in with physical exercises.

FOR PMR: Take in a deep breathe, tense up, and breathe out as you let go.
FOR STRETCHING: Slowly breath in as you begin a stretch. Slowly breathe out as you unstretch.

Step 4: Type Exercise Instructions in Script

Using your checklist, go pack to the early chapters in this book that actually present the instructions for each exercise. Then copy the instructions for each exercise either on some 3" X 5"cards or into your computer. For example, if you selected the "Arm Squeeze" exercise from progressive muscle relaxation, you would type in the complete instructions:

Arm Squeeze

    Touch the palm of your right hand to your right shoulder. Your arm should be bending at the elbow. Tense up your arm. Hold to the tension to the count of five. Let go and go completely limp. Count to twenty while letting the muscles get more and more relaxed.

Step 5: Connect your exercises with phrases suggesting a unifying idea.

Here's where you get creative. In order for your sequence to be more than a boring jumble of exercises, you want to think of theme that connects them. Here is an example of some exercises without a unifying idea (Smith, 2005):

YOGA
    Slowly, smoothly, and gently raise your arms high in the air.
    Higher and higher, until they are stretching all the way. Hold the stretch.
    Then slowly, smoothly, and gently unstretch.
BREATHING
    Slowly take in a deep breath, filling your abdomen with air.
    And gently exhale through your lips, very smoothly and gently.
IMAGERY
    Imagine a beautiful tree.
    You can hear a breeze flow through the leaves, feel the wind touch your skin, and smell the gentle fragrance of leave.
MEDITATION
    Very gently rock back and forth. Attend only to your rocking motion.

Notice how these exercises are disconnected. Here is the same sequence with a unifying idea, such as the image of a tree swaying in the wind.

    Imagine you are a tree gently swaying in the wind. Your arms are like branches. The wind begins to blow against your branches and they begin to move.

YOGA
    Slowly, smoothly, and gently raise your arms high in the air.
    Higher and higher, until they are stretching all the way. Hold the stretch.

Then slowly, smoothly, and gently unstretch.
The wind begins to subside into a gentle breeze. The flow of air is a gentle as your breath. As you easily breathe in, you gentle breeze touches your nose. As you breathe out, air flows out into the breeze.
BREATHING
Slowly take in a deep breath, filling your abdomen with air.
Pause.
And gently exhale through your lips, very smoothly and gently.
The breeze has become even more quiet.
IMAGERY
You can hear a breeze flow through the leaves, feel the wind touch your skin, and smell the gentle fragrance of leave.
MEDITATION
Very gently rock back and forth. Attend only to your rocking motion.
And now the air is almost completely silent. And the tree very slowly rocks   back and forth as the air gently touches its branches.
In the following segment the unifying idea is "breathing out tension and settling into calm."

First think of a unifying idea. Then think of how it is related to each type of exercise you have selected. How does it connect your exercises. Then, insert phrases for each group of exercises that mention the unifying idea. When using cards, write in the phrases.

Step 6: Spice It Up with R-States

If you have completed the six approaches to relaxation, you should have R-State Questionnaires for each. Select which R-State words you like for each exercise. If you checked the words "energized," "refreshed," and "aware" for yoga, then use these words. If you checked "distant," "warm," and "calm" for progressive muscle relaxation, select these words.

Once you have selected words for each group of exercises, insert these words in the instructions in your script. For example, imagine you have selected the Arm Squeeze exercise from progressive muscle relaxation and like the words "warm," "heavy," and "at ease." Would then insert these words in your selected exercise, perhaps like this:

Arm Squeeze

Touch the palm of your right hand to your right shoulder. Your arm should be bending at the elbow. Tense up your arm. Hold to the tension to the count of five. Let go and go completely limp. FEEL WARM AND HEAVY. Count to twenty while letting the muscles get more and more relaxed. LET YOURSELF FEEL AT EASE

Step 7: Record your Modified Instructions

You are now just about finished. Read your instructions into a tape recorder or other recording device. You might want to select some quiet background nature sounds, or a background recording of peaceful music. When making your recording, you don't have to worry about being an accomplished actor. Just say the words, and let the words have their effect. However, keep two very important points in mind:

- SPEAK VERY SLOWLY!!
- INTRODUCE LOTS OF PAUSES. PAUSE ABOUT THREE SECONDS AFTER EVERY SENTENCE OR TWO.

Example of a Complete Exercise Sequence

In this example it is easy to see which exercises were selected. Examine this script closely and try to answer these questions:

1. Why were the exercises presented in this order (rather than, for example, putting meditation and imagery at the beginning?)
2. How was the unifying idea mentioned throughout the sequence?
3. Can you find the R-State words?

UNIFYING IDEA: RELAXING ON THE BEACH

Imagine you are resting on your back on the beach. A leafy palm tree overhead filters the sun. You begin to relax.

Arm and Side Stretch

Start with both arms resting by your sides. Slowly, smoothly and gently circle your right arm and hand up towards your head, then over your head. like the hand of a clock or the wing of a bird. Very slowly, moving through the sand. Reach all the way , arching your back. Then gently return your arm. Imagine your arms sinking in the sand. The feel very calm and at ease.

Front of Neck Stretch

Let your head tilt, this time backward, letting gravity do the work. Feel the front of your neck stretch..You can feel your head pressing into the sand.
Let gravity pull your head back

Arm Squeeze

Touch the palm of your right hand to your right shoulder. Your arm should be bending at the elbow. [BREATHE IN THROUGH YOUR LIPS] Tense up your arm. Hold to the tension to the count of five. [BREATHE OUT THROUGH YOUR LIPS AS YOU LET GO] Let go

and go completely limp. Count to twenty while letting the
muscles get more and more relaxed. Let your arms sink into the
soothing and comfortable beach sand. You feel so at ease. So
peaceful.

Shoulder Squeeze

[BREATHE IN] Shrug the shoulders, lifting them up.
[BREATHE OUT] Let go and go completely limp for about
20 seconds. Tension dissolves and flows into the sand.
You feel deeply at ease.

Back of Neck Squeeze.

[BREATHE IN] Gently tilt the head back, creating a
slight squeeze in the muscles in the back of the neck.
[BREATHE OUT] Let go and go completely limp for about
20 seconds.

Leg Squeeze

[BREATHE IN] Pull your right leg back pressing it
against the sand. Feel the tension all along your leg up
through the buttocks. [BREATHE OUT] Let go and go
completely limp for about 20 seconds. Your legs sink into
the sand. Very comfortable and relaxed. Very soothed.

Warmth and Heaviness

Hands and arms, warm and heavy. Like resting in the
sun. Like feeling warm water. Like magnets are pulling
them down. Tension dissolves and flows away. You feel
distant and far away. Indifferent. Repeat for legs and feet.

Blowing and Breathing

Take a slow deep breath and pause. Breathe out
slowly though your lips, as if you were blowing at a leaf
floating in front of you, just enough to make the leaf stay in
the air, but now blow away. Breathe in through your nose.
You feel at each and calm with every breath. Imagine you
are easily blowing on the clouds above.
Imagery

Imagine relaxing on a peaceful beach. You see the
blue sky above You feel the warm sun on your sink. The
water is a beautiful blue, reflecting the clouds above. You
see a gentle ripple from the breeze. In the distance are
boats slowly floating across the horizon. You hear the
splashing waves in the distance. You feel peaceful and
filled with joy. You smell the clean scent of water . . .

Meditation

Attend to the sound of the waves. This is your
meditation. Simply attend to this sound. Whenever your
mind wanders, gently return, again and again and again.

CHAPTER 13
SPOT RELAXATION

When you wake up from sleep, perhaps you stretch. After moving heavy furniture, perhaps you rub your arms. These are examples of **spot relaxation**, one of the most useful applications of the approaches taught in this book. Spot relaxation is a 1-5 minute relaxation exercise targeted to a specific problem or goal. Once you have learned the six families of relaxation in this book (which I recommend before trying this chapter), you have a rich source of possible types of spot relaxation. Simply take one or two exercises and try them in a situation that might call for relaxation.

It can be particularly effective to combine exercises. For example, if your neck is stiff after a hour of typing, you might first practice the neck squeeze from progressive muscle relaxation followed by the yogaform stretching neck stretch. Here are some suggestions:

- Progressive muscle relaxation (PMR) and autogenic warmth and heaviness exercises evoke somatic sensations and can be combined and sequenced: "Tense up . . . let go . . . feel warm and heavy as the tension flows away."
- Autogenic exercises work best after PMR or breathing, and may be combined with imagery.
- PMR and imagery can be designed to both target muscles.
- PMR and breathing exercises both directly instruct one to "let go" or "release." Combination option: "Breathe in . . tense up . . and as you let go, exhale, letting the air easily flow through your lips."
- PMR and stretching both involve movement of muscles. Combination option: "Tense up your fingers and make a fist. Release the tension. Then slowly stretch open your fingers all the way, and slowly release the stretch."
- Passive breathing exercises can be combined with any other family of techniques.
- PMR and imagery can both target muscles. Combination option: "Tense up your muscles,

as if you were squeezing a wad of paper. Let go, and let the wad of paper slowly relax and open."
- Yoga stretching and rocking meditation can involve movement of the torso. Combination option: "Bow over and stretch your back . . . reach up to the sky . . . and now sit and gently rock back and forth, attending to your rocking movement."
- Imagery and autogenic visual suggestions are both visual. Combination option: "Imagine relaxing on a beach. You can see the soft clouds, hear waves, and smell the clean water. The sun touches your skin, you feel warm and heavy."

The possibilities for spot relaxation and nearly endless. Here are some examples. Read them, then see what you can think of.

Situation: *I work in a day care center and spend lots of time holding the kids. This wears me out, especially when a child starts crying in my arms.*
Spot relaxation: *I gently rock a child while I breathe slowly and evenly. I try to pace my rocking with my breathing. This has a way of calming both the baby and me.*

Situation: *I am at my dentist's for a filling. Usually, the drilling and poking in my mouth makes me very tense.*
Spot relaxation: *I imagine a cool ice cube touching my gums and cheeks. That seems to take away the discomfort.*

Situation: *I drive several hours a day, two and from work. After a long drive, my shoulders and arms are very knotted up.*
Spot relaxation: *PMR Shoulder squeeze followed by yogaform shoulder stretch.*

Situation: *I go to my doctor's office twice a month for a blood test. The idea of sticking me with a needle really upsets me. Here's what I do.*
Spot relaxation: *I imagine myself at a peaceful, far away island. I think of a friendly little monkey grabbing*

on my arm where I am actually getting stuck. This way I turn the sensations of getting stuck into sensations of being grabbed.

Situation: *When driving home, I often get stuck in a traffic jam. For about 30 minutes everyone moves very slowly. Usually, my temper rises and my arms get very tense.*

Spot relaxation: *I see how slowly and evenly I can breathe. When I breathe out, I let go of tension in my arms.*

Situation: *In the middle of the morning, after reading many reports, I need a refresher break.*

Spot relaxation: *I close my eyes and meditate for about 5 minutes.*

CHAPTER 13 EXERCISES
---

1. Your Spot Relaxation Exercises

Experiment with different types and combinations of spot relaxation. Over the week see if you can think of something different for six situations.

Situation
Spot Relaxation

Situation
Spot Relaxation

Situation
Spot Relaxation

Situation
Spot Relaxation

Situation
Spot Relaxation

PART III
PROBLEM-SOLVING

CHAPTER 14
THE FAST-TRACK TO PROBLEM-SOLVING

Stress is a problem to be solved. It is the philosophy of this book that no matter how bad or how impossible things may seem, there is something that can be done about it. Perhaps it's not the ideal solution. But it may be the best you can expect. It may address only part of what's wrong. But Rome was not built in a day. And from your efforts you may develop important skills for dealing with future problems.

An important part of solving a problem quickly and efficiently is coming up with a good definition of what's wrong. First, we will consider mistakes that are often made.

Vague, Over-Emotional, Distorted Definitions

Below are examples of various individuals under stress. In each example, the person knows there's a problem and is trying to define it clearly.

Bart has no girlfriend and is feeling lonely. He desperately wants to meet people. How Bart defines his problem: "Everyone keeps to themselves. No one likes to talk to people anymore. People are too selfish."

Bart's definition doesn't get to what the real problem is, how to meet people. His definition is actually a distorted view of the world. Realistically, it is just not true that *everyone* keeps to themselves or that *no one* likes to talk to people. His complaint that people are too selfish sounds too overemotional to be helpful.

Eloise has planned a month-long vacation with her boyfriend. Suddenly, her mother comes down with a serious illness, and Eloise must stay with her to help her recover. How Eloise defines her problem: "This is the worst thing that could ever happen to me. This is an absolute disaster. Everything's ruined. I give up."

Eloise's definition of her problem is so emotional she can barely figure out what her options

are. And surely she is exaggerating and distorting things by seeing her predicament as an absolute disaster. And it is vague.

Abdul is a convenience store manager and is having a bad week. Food deliveries are late, there's not enough change in the cash register, his daughter is sick and needs attention, and he has supplied his store with too many eggs. Abdul's problem-definition: "Everything is happening at once. I feel like a wall of rocks has just crumbled down on me and there's nothing I can do."

This definition is also very emotional and vague.

When faced with a challenge, often our first reaction is emotional outburst. That can be very healthy and motivate us to get to work, communicate to potential helpers the seriousness of our predicament, and release tension. However, it is important to realize that our initial outburst is not the same as a good problem-definition. That may come next, once the air has cleared.

Fast-Track Problem Definitions

A fast-track problem-definition goes beyond one's initial emotional, vague, and distorted outburst. You select a stress situation and then consider the following three questions as concretely as possible :

1. What do you ideally want?
2. What part can you realistically get for now?
3. When and where can you start?

What do you ideally want? Think of what is causing stress in your life. Now, identify what you really want. Describe your ideal want in positive rather than negative terms, for example:

Negative want: To get people to ignore me less.
Positive version: To meet more people

Negative want: Be less poor
Positive version: To find ways of making money.

Negative want: Stop messing up at school
Positive version: Improve my grades.

What Can You Realistically Get for Now?
Very often, when we think of a positive outcome we might want in a stress situation, we ask for too much. The following wants may be quite laudable and desirable, but none can be realistically achieved in a day or two.

> *Find a job that really fits my needs and abilities in my*
> *   neighborhood.*
> *Find a boyfriend who shares my interests in music and*
> *   Chinese food.*
> *Get a passing grade in my math class.*
> *Work more efficiently, so I have fewer projects to take*
> *   home.*
> *Get my two kids to stop fighting.*
> *Figure out how to balance the demands of work,*
> *   school, and play.*
> *Get thin with nice muscle definition.*
> *Get enough money to pay for school and my car.*

People sometimes fall into the trap of not identifying subgoals that must be achieved before seeking their identified stress-management goals. One step in identifying what you can realistically get for now is identifying any prerequisite subgoals. If there is a subgoal, make that your "goal for now."

Let's illustrate this with one of the above examples, a student who has identified as his goal, "Getting a passing grade in my math class." She quickly identified the immediate task that had to be confronted, what she could realistically try to get for now: "Getting a better grade on my daily homework assignments." And when our student focused on this realistic goal, she quickly realized she needed a subgoal, "Finding a quiet place, conducive to study, where I can work on my homework an hour every evening."

What, when, and where can you start? It is easy to get stuck at the stage of identifying a specific, realistic goal. A useful sign that you are on the right track is if your goal is defined in terms of specific deeds or words you will do or say, in a specific time and place – what, when, and where. Our previous student has made real progress by defining her problem in terms of finding a study environment. She can fine-tune this definition by answering the "what, when, and where" questions.

What? I want to sit in front of a desk with my book in front of me so I can read my assignment and complete the homework.
When? I need to figure out how to study sometime every evening, preferably 7-9 PM.
Where? The place has to be quiet, with few distractions.

Bart, Eloise, and Abdul – Problems Redefined

Let's return to the three individuals we met at the start of this chapter, Bart, Eloise, and Abdul. Here is how they redefined their problems in terms of the concepts of this chapter. Can you see how each concept was applied?

Bart. "*Eventually I want a girlfriend, but that can't happen overnight. I need to start socializing more, but that too takes time. I can at least figure out where I might meet people, for example, at the temple, the local coffee house, or in my dorm. Here's what I'll do. Before Friday this week I will make a point of introducing myself to at least three women, and ask at least one if they might be interested in having a coffee with me. That's a step.*"

Eloise. "*My mother is sick and I have to stay home rather than go on my vacation with my boyfriend. Sure, that's frustration, even a downer. But it isn't the end of the world. My boyfriend will understand. I'll get together with him tonight and we can discuss this predicament. By putting our heads together we can come up with a solution.*"

Abdul. "*It seems like everything is happening at once at the store I manage. Late deliveries, too many eggs on stock, and my sick daughter. I sure wish my problems wouldn't come all at once! Well, something has to be done. I need to start chipping away at this mess. I'll be prioritize, figure out what has to be done now, and do one job at a time. I'll start now.*"

CHAPTER 14 EXERCISES

1. Fixing troubled problem-definitions

Below are some examples of problem definitions. For each, identify what's wrong with the definition. Which of the following steps is missing?

1. What the person ideally wants
2. What part can the person realistically get for now
3. When and where can the person have a reasonable chance of getting it.

Then offer your suggestion of a better definition, and explain how it incorporates each of the above steps.

PROBLEM

I do not want the traffic situation not to be so bad when I'm going to work. There's so much traffic that I get really upset and tense. Sometimes I have to wait 20 minutes in a traffic jam going nowhere. This really upsets me for the entire day!

WHAT'S WRONG WITH THIS DEFINITION

YOUR IMPROVED VERSION

PROBLEM

Every time we have a weekly church meeting, I am voted to be the secretary. This upsets me, especially when I have important other things to do. My problem is this: I want people to respect me more and pay more attention to my needs.

WHAT'S WRONG WITH THIS DEFINITION

YOUR IMPROVED VERSION

2. Your Problem-Definitions

This week, identify some stressful situations or events.
Then define each in terms of a problem

Describe the stressful situation or event

What do you ideally want?

What part can you realistically get for now?

What, when, and where can you start?

Describe the stressful situation or event

What do you ideally want?

What part can you realistically get for now?

What, when, and where can you start?

CHAPTER 15
BRAINSTORMING YOUR WAY TO SUCCESS

Harry has a specific stress management goal: How to get his supervisor to recognize his work accomplishments. One day during a coffee break it comes to him: "I'll list my accomplishments on a bright pink sticky note, which I will then affix to the monthly report I turn in. That's it!"

This may seem like a perfectly sensible solution to a problem. It is not particularly vague, overemotional, or distorted. It identifies a specific course of action. But there is a problem, one that limits the success of many attempts at stress management. Harry jumped on the first idea that came to mind, treated it as "The Answer," and proceeded to act. If you think about it, surely Harry could have thought of something better than pink sticky notes!

The chances for successful stress management increase when we maximize our choices. Quantity yields quality. This requires that we pause, generate many options, and carefully weed out the good from the bad. In this chapter we consider the venerable problem-solving tool of brainstorming.

Brainstorming involves putting aside efforts to judge, criticize, and analyze. Instead, you let the ideas flow, without censorship. Because you do this without censorship, you let all ideas come, the good, the bad, and the silly. Your goal is to whatever needed to uncork an "idea fountain." Then, after the flood, you sort out your options and make a choice.

Starting the Brainstorming Idea Fountain

It can be frustrating to start the brainwashing idea fountain. Imagine you re an executive employed at a large cardboard box factory. You're at a very important business meeting, sitting at a huge, heavy oak table. Everyone is in a nicely pressed suit facing each other. The agenda is long and tedious. After two hours, your group reaches agenda item number 9 – how to increase sales. The problem is that more and more people are using plastic bags, resulting in a business decline for many types of boxes. One person suggests, "Lets brainstorm!" People agree that this is a good idea.

Then for the next five minutes everyone sits like frogs on a log, staring into space. Cautiously, someone suggests, "well, we could do better at advertising." Another comments, "Yes, and we could cut our cell phone use." Another idea: "Maybe we could work six days a week." Clearly, this is going nowhere. The idea fountain is stuck or clogged. The lesson is that brainstorming just doesn't happen; it needs proper preparation and the proper setting. Our corporate table isn't quite right. And the suits don't help. Here are some suggestions:

- Set a brainstorming time and place apart from one's usual work or study environment. Take away reminders to be critical and serious. Have fun!

- Prepare for brainstorming with a little relaxation, possibly deep breathing followed by imagery. This can help reduce interfering tension and foster a creative set of mind.

Enhancing Variety

Although brainstorming calls for temporarily putting aside critical thinking, sometimes that isn't enough to ensure variety. Try these tools:

- First brainstorm general categories of solutions. Then treat each category as a separate brainstorming task. For example, let's return to our cardboard box problem. Your task is to brainstorm unusual product uses for cardboard boxes. Variety can be increased by first brainstorming categories:

Structures	*Toys*
Tools	*Wacky Ideas*

One then brainstorms possibilities for each category:

Structures: *a cardboard house, church, skyscraper, doghouse, fish tank, birdhouse*
Tools: *a big cardboard shovel, a step, a torch,*

emergency clothing, cement shaper

Toys: *Mr. Squarepants, a toy dog, a square pumpkin face, a drawing board with four sides, something to kick in kickball, a target*

Wacky Ideas: *An emergency outdoor bathtub, an unexpected place to hide valuables, wax it and make it a boat, a very thin box could be a hot-air balloon, a place to store laughs (?)*

• Visualize a similar problem situation, one not exactly the same, that you have faced. Brainstorm for that situation. See if any of the applications suggest your original problem. For example, if you are having trouble thinking of uses for cardboard boxes, think of a similar problem, perhaps uses for string. You may think of the following:

> *Tie pets together with string when outside.*
> *Weave into a loose pair of gloves to cover fingers*
> *Wrap your hands so you can pick up hot objects without getting burned.*
> *Drape them over a pond to begin making a bridge.*
> *Mash them up, mix with water and glue, and make a paste for sculptures.*

Some of these same ideas can transfer to cardboard boxes:

> *Store pets in big boxes outside.*
> *Put small boxes over your fingers to you can pick up hot objects*
> *Glue them over a pond to make a bridge*
> *Mash them up, mix with water, and make a paste for sculptures.*

Making a choice

After brainstorming, you need to make a selection. First, cross out all of the ideas that are very unrealistic. Then pick 3 - 5 ideas that are the best. For each, do a "cost-benefit" analysis. That is, for each idea list all the negatives or costs in one column, and all the positives or benefits in another. Then rank your best ideas.

CHAPTER 15 EXERCISES

1. Brainstorming practice

Imagine you own a business that manufactures plastic dolls. Your dolls are something like the popular "Barbie" product. One day your major factory goofed up and produced thousands of dolls with something of a defect. You see, the robotic hair-gluing machine accidentally glued hair to each doll's feet, and none to the top of their heads, resulting in thousands of inflatable bald dolls with hairy feet. Because of the upcoming holiday season, you simply do not have time to order a new set of dolls. And that would be far too expensive. Your only solution is creative marketing. How can you package these "defective" dolls so that they are actually "desirable"? This is your brainstorming task.

If you are in a group, divide the group into two subgroups. Group 1 has this task:

> Brainstorm ways of packaging and marketing Blow-up Barb. However, do not use the "brainstorm categories" option.

Group 2 has a slightly different task:

> First brainstorm categories of uses. Then for each category, brainstorm solutions.

At the end of this exercise, groups compare their responses. Discuss the advantages and disadvantages of category brainstorming.

If you are not in a group, try brainstorming first without categories. Then repeat the exercise using categories. Compare your responses.

2. Pick a Problem to Brainstorm

Select a problem you have faced in the past. Make it as specific and concrete as possible. Brainstorm possible solutions. Do a cost / benefit analysis of the five best option.

CHAPTER 16
TIME MANAGEMENT: THE DAY INVENTORY

One of the most general problems people face is finding time. A busy schedule, competing demands, and unexpected emergencies can add up to a chaotic day. You may not complete all you want, or leave important tasks half done. And in spite of your efforts, you may end the day frustrated and fatigued.

Alan Lakein (1973) and Harold Greenwald (1973) have offered useful time management ideas that are frequently cited in the literature. Here are some of their ideas.

A good step in managing time is to take time off and complete a day inventory. Such an inventory can pinpoint where are you spending too much time, and what tasks are getting shortchanged. It is a good way of identifying time-busters, unnecessary activities that can eat up minutes and hours.

We will consider as our example, Greta a college student. When asked how she spends her time, she suggested, "I think I spend too much time walking the dog and eating." We will show how Greta completed her day inventory task.

Your Current Schedule

How do you spend your day? Divide your day into half-hour periods and record your activities for each. Here is Greta's day:

Greta's Day

8:30-9:00	Eat breakfast
9:00-9:30	Eat breakfast
9:30-10:00	Surf the internet
10:00-10:30	Accounting Class
10:30-11:00	Accounting Class
11:00-11:30	Class
11:30-12:00	Walk the dog
12:30-1:00	Listen to the radio
1:00-1:30	Snack
1:30-2:00	Watch TV
2:00-2:30	Part-time job
2:30-3:00	Part-time job
3:00-3:30	Part-time job

3:30-4:00	Part-time job
4:00-4:30	Take a walk
4:30-5:00	Read magazines
5:00-5:30	Study by self
5:30-6:00	Doing homework with friends
6:00-6:30	Dinner
6:30-7:00	Dinner
7:00-7:30	Play video
7:30-8:00	Watch TV
8:00-8:30	Call mom
8:30-9:00	Study
9:00-9:30	Talk with friends
9:30-10:00	Study
10:00-10:30	Watch the news
10:30-11:00	Get ready for bed

At first there may seem to be nothing unusual with this log. However, if we look at it with a microscope, some suspicious things emerge. This involves first involves sorting the days activities into different categories. Create 5 - 10 general categories that represent what you have been doing. Greta listed the following:

What Greta Does: Categories

Eating and snacking
Studying
Work
In class
Socializing on phone
Recreation (TV, radio, video games)
Chores
Getting ready for bed, dressing, etc.

Now, add up how much time you devote to each category of activity. Greta discovered she devoted her day to the following activities:

Time Greta Spends on Each Activity

Summary

2 ½ hr	Eating and snacking
2 hr	Studying
2 hr	Work
1 ½ hr	In class
1 hr	Socializing on phone
4 hr	Recreation (TV, radio, video games)
½ hr	Chores
½ hr	Getting ready for bed, dressing, etc.

By examining this summary chart, you can consider four important time management questions:

1. Are you spending too much time on some activities?
2. Have you organized your day in the most reasonable way?
3. Have you scheduled in times for fun and recreation? Put these after a challenging and difficult activities, to reward yourself and help recover completely.
4. Have you scheduled your most demanding mental tasks for when you are most awake, your "prime time."

Greta was surprised that she spent 4 hours a day in recreation, 2 ½ hours eating and snacking, and only ½ hour on chores. She decided to cut down on her recreation, or at least put off some of these activities to the weekend. She also decided to put her "fun time" right after work or study, as a kind of reward. She gets more studying done if she studies in one block of time, rather than breaking up, so she scheduled one large block of evening time for study.

Work Schedules vs. Personal Schedules

In this age of personal data assistants and pocket-sized leather schedule books, making a schedule is easy. Or so it might seem. There is one reason why schedules often fail. Here's an example. Ray is an undergraduate studying math. He also works in the school cafeteria. This semester he is taking a full load of classes and is quite busy. He decided he needed to carefully complete a schedule, but it didn't work out. Here's his account:

I have so much work to do! It seems overwhelming! Well, let's get down to business. I get up at 6, get ready, and arrive at my first class at 7. The class

goes until 10. I study from 10 to 12 and then grab a quick lunch. At 12:30 I run off to work and clean dishes for two hours. My next class is at 3:30 and is over at 5:30. I grab some food and by 6 go off to the library to write some papers for English. And 8 I begin reading my math assignment and from 10 to 11 do my math homework. Then I go to bed.

Can you see any problem with this schedule? Here's Ray's account:

Well, this schedule worked for two days, then it fell apart. I got so caught up in my obligations that I forgot to put in time for myself, God, my friends, and, most important, my boyfriend Chris. I had created an all-work schedule. It might have worked for a robot, but not for me.

Ray's story illustrates a problem many face when creating schedules. Often we are prompted to write a schedule because of too much serious work. So when we write a schedule our minds are on our work, and we forget the rest of life. To avoid this problem, let me suggest an exercise: first create a **work schedule**, one that includes all the things you have to do – your job, school, personal hygiene, cleaning your room, and so on. Then create your **personal schedule**, one that includes all the things you do for yourself and do with friends and those close to you. Then compare your two schedules. Often you may have to make some compromises in both. Your final schedule contains both what you have to do and your personal schedule.

CHAPTER 16 EXERCISES

1. How you spend your time

Complete a time schedule, using the instructions in this chapter. When your schedule is completed, identify any activities that may be taking up too much time.

2. Analyze your time

Look at your response to 1. Consider these questions:

1. Are you spending too much time on some activities?
2. Have you organized your day in the most reasonable way?
3. Have you scheduled in times for fun and recreation? Put these after a challenging and difficult activities, to reward yourself and help recover completely.
4. Have you scheduled your most demanding mental tasks for when you are most awake, your "prime time."

3. Your work, personal, and compromise schedules

Work schedule. First, list all of the things you have to do today, your work obligations. This includes your job and school as well as the necessities of taking care of yourself like eating, brushing your teeth, cleaning your room, and so on. Put these activities in a "work schedule."

Personal schedule. Now, put your work schedule aside. Forget about it for a minute. Then list the personal and people-related activities you want to do today. Put them in your "personal schedule."

Compromise schedule. Finally, look at both your work and personal schedules. Where do they conflict? Where can you compromise?

What was the most difficult challenge in creating a compromise schedule?

CHAPTER 17
PRIORITIES AND GOALS

Difficulties with managing time can be a symptom of unclear and conflicting goals and priorities. Alan Lakein (1973) and Harold Greenwald (1973) offer some useful ideas we will consider in this chapter.

Different people value different things. Some may want a life of adventure, others money, others a good family, and still others artistic expression. Your goals reflect what truly matter and how you wish to spend your time. However, sometimes we get sidetracked and find ourselves wasting time on pursuits that do not meet our goals. Sometimes we get in habitual daily patterns in which we waste time with tasks that do not fit our priorities. In this chapter, we take a look at priorities and goals.

Long-Term Goals

First, what are your long-term goals? Try thinking at three levels: lifetime goals, five-year goals, and six-month goals. Here are some examples of each:

Life-time goals
To get married and have children, no more than six.
To get a stable and enjoyable job.
To find a place to settle down on the coast.

Five-year goals
To start and finish college
To try at least two jobs
To get married

Six-month goals
To get into a good college and have a good first year.
To take dating more seriously, and look for a mate

Identify Six-Month Subgoals and Tasks

Your six-month goals are ones you need to start working on right away, Consider each, and ask what important subgoals are involved. What tasks have to be completed? For example, the six-month goals can be broken down like this:

Getting into a good college
Study for college exams
Keep my grades up
Look for people to write letters of recommendation

Taking dating more seriously
Look over my list of friends and ask if any are potentials for dating
Review my socializing "hangouts" and identify any that are not good places to meet people to date
Think of some quality time activities I could spend with my date.

Identify Activities that may be Interfering with you r Goals

Can you think of any activities that are reducing your chances of completing your goals? Be realistic. Obviously, everything you do can't be goal-oriented. You need some unscheduled fun time. However, if your goal is to get into college, habitually missing class can get in the way. If you want to increase your chances of finding a spouse, spending all your time alone isn't helping.

Identify Goals and Activities for This Week. . . then Today

Lakein suggests first thinking of your week, and then today, as filing cabinets with three drawers. In your "top drawer" put your most important priorities and goals, those that absolutely, positively, must be done this week or today. In the "middle drawer" include activities it would be nice to complete, but can be temporarily postponed until you complete your top drawer activities. Bottom drawer priorities can be put off until last, until you have extra time. To this filing cabinet, lets add a waste basket, or using today's computer lingo, a "recycle bin." In your recycle bin put activities you need to cut down on or cease, because they are just a waste.

Here's an example:

<u>*This Week's Filing Cabinet*</u>

<u>*Top Drawer*</u>
    Getting an A on my exams and homework
    Spending a least some good time with my date
<u>*Middle Drawer*</u>
    Having fun playing basketball
    Writing letters
<u>*Bottom Drawer*</u>
    Perfecting my video game
<u>*Recycle Bin*</u>
    Looking for and test driving a new car, even though
    I can't buy one

<u>*Today's filing cabinet*</u>

<u>*Top Drawer*</u>
    Finish English assignment; ask my English major
    friend read it for errors.

<u>*Middle Drawer*</u>
    Schedule my date.
<u>*Bottom Drawer*</u>
    Write my Mom
<u>*Recycle Bin*</u>
    Going through ads for new cars

What Makes you Really Happy and Satisfied

Now that you have done some structured review of your goals and activities, it is time to sit back and give them one more review. This time simply ask yourself the Big Question: What do you really want in life? Imagine you are in a time machine and go many years, even decades into the future. From this special perspective you can see all that you have done. Then ask, "What might I have done differently? What is really important to me?"

CHAPTER 17 EXERCISES

---

1. What are your long-term goals?

2. What are your six month subgoals and tasks?

3. What activities may be interfering with your goals?

4. For this week, identify:

Top Drawer Priorities and Goals

Middle Drawer Priorities and Goals

Bottom Drawer Priorities and Goals

Recycle Bin Priorities and Goals

5 For today, identify

Top Drawer Priorities and Goals

Middle Drawer Priorities and Goals

Bottom Drawer Priorities and Goals

Recycle Bin Priorities and Goals

6   What makes you really happy and satisfied?   Which goals contribute to this?

CHAPTER 18
DEALING WITH PROCRASTINATION

The procrastinator experiences a special type of stress – avoiding a task they have chosen to do. People sometimes avoid activities they actually enjoy; however, it is more common to procrastinate with tasks that may have a long-term or delayed payoff. Procrastination is especially likely when there is possible payoff to avoidance or delay.

Identify Short-Term Delay Tricks

Sometimes we procrastinate through delay tricks, by focusing on short-term payoffs while ignoring long-term benefits. Simply identifying your delay tricks can clarify your choices – are the immediate rewards worth putting long-term rewards in jeopardy? Some short-term delay tricks might include:

• Maybe someone else will do the task.
• It feels goods to avoid potential failure.
• Maybe the problem will just solve itself.
• Maybe it will be easier or lest costly to do the task later.
• Putting off a task is a way of "getting even," or showing others indirectly how you feel.

Which fit you? Which are unrealistic? Can you identify specific times and places you use these delay tricks.

Procrastination Triggers and Environments

We are more likely to procrastinate when in a setting that encourages putting things off. If you are living with three party-going roommates, you might find it difficult to get serious work done because of the constant temptation to go partying. If you work next to the coffee machine, you might be tempted to put tasks off in order to take another coffee break. In identifying procrastination triggers, you need to specify:

1. What didn't get done.
2. What distracted you.

Sometimes one's environment is simply not conducive to the task at hand, and is more conducive to some other activity. Examples include:

Filing out tax forms in the TV room (rather than a quiet, serious study room)
Writing a serious letter while in a restaurant.
Planning a family budget at lunch.

The following questions can help you consider whether the environment is contributing to procrastination.

1. What didn't you get done?
2. Where were you procrastinating?
3. How was this environment conducive to another, competing activity?

Simplify Difficult Jobs

Sometimes people procrastinate when confronting a task that is seen as too big or challenging. Burns (1990) emphasizes making a job easy, either by breaking it down into logical steps or completing work in "small spurts." Here one commits to doing say fifteen or thirty minutes of a task (no more) a day, until it is done. The advantage of the small spurt approach is that it frees one from worrying about how a task when viewed as a whole might be overwhelming. Another approach is to simply break a job down into component parts, and take on one part at a time.

TIC-TOC and Distorted Thoughts

Ferrari, Johnson, and McCown (1995) suggest a number of types of distorted thinking about a task that can lead to procrastination. Do you display any of these?

• Overestimating the amount of time or work required for a task.
• Overestimating future motivational states ("I'll feel like doing this later");

- Assuming that success at a task requires one be in a positive task-oriented mood and "feel smart, motivated, awake, and calm";
- Assuming that task failure or reduced productivity is the result of lack of lack of such states;
- Assuming one must be perfect;
- Thinking everything one does should go easily and without effort;
- Believing that if it's not done right, it's not worth doing at all;
- Assuming there is one right answer, and one should wait until they find it.

Aaron Beck (1993) has invented a useful and popular tool for dealing with such procrastinating distortions. He calls it the "TIC-TOC Technique."
First you identify Task-Interfering Cognitions ("TICs"), perhaps among those listed above. Then think of improved replacement thoughts, or Task-Oriented Cognitions ("TOCs"). Here are some TIC-TOCs:

TIC: *I can't begin this work until I am sure I will do it to near perfection.*
TOC: *I can't tell how this work will go until I begin. Once I'm into it, I can decide what more needs to be done.*

TIC: *This problem will just solve itself if I just wait.*
TOC: *Realistically, the problem won't go away, and it may get worse.*

TIC: *I shouldn't being doing this task until I am in the right mood.*
TOC: *Sometimes everyone has to complete chores that are less than pleasant. There is no reason why I should be different.*

CHAPTER 18 EXERCISES

1. Short-Term Rewards and Delay Tricks

List some specific tasks you put off this week. Specify exactly what the task was, and when and where you attempted to complete it.

What possible short-term rewards and delay tricks contributed to your procrastination for the above activities?

2. Procrastination Triggers and Environments

Describe your favorite procrastination triggers. What environments are most likely to foster procrastination for you?

3. TIC-TOC

Select a task you have been putting off. What are your TICS (Task-Interfering Cognitions)?
What are your TOCS (Task-Orienting Cognitions)?

WHAT YOU PROCRASTINATED	TICS Task-Interfering Cognitions	TOCS Task-Orienting Cognitions

PART IV
THINKING
REALISTICALLY

CHAPTER 19
HIDDEN STRESS-PRODUCING THOUGHTS

I just don't see how my thinking contributes to stress. It seems so obvious. I get a flat tire. I get upset, and that's it. My daughter doesn't return my car on time, and that makes me angry. My doctor says I have a condition, and I get depressed. Bad things cause me to get upset. A causes B.

Sometimes situations are so bad that it's hard not to blame them entirely for the distress they seem to cause. And sometimes our distress is so intense that it's easy to look for some outside cause. Indeed, our first impulse when something goes wrong is often to look for an outside culprit.

Yet our thoughts, our cognitions, can play a crucial role. Sometimes this is clear when we compare two versions of the same problem:

Todd has just broken up with his girlfriend of two years. He is taking it very hard. He finds it hard to sleep each night and feels depressed and anxious. He is bothered by stomach distress. When discussing his breakup, he complains "This was my only chance to make a relationship work. This breakup proves that I don't have what it takes to find a girl. I'm a looser."

Ted has also broken up with his girlfriend of two years. However, he isn't taking it so hard. He sleeps just fine, and goes on with his day. When discussing his breakup, he explains, "Sure, the breakup was a disappointment. But it wasn't the end of the world. Life goes on. You learn from your mistakes."

Tod and Ted have experienced a breakup, but Tod is distressed, whereas Ted is mildly upset.. The reason for the difference is obvious. Tod is worrying unnecessarily. He is taking things too hard. He is making an unfortunate situation worse. In other words, he is thinking himself into stress.

Whatever stress situation you may be experiencing, imagine that somewhere there is a Ted (or Tina) in the same predicament. However, they are not as upset. The difference is that your less-stress Ted / Tina is not thinking stressful thoughts.

One popular way of uncovering hidden thoughts or cognitions is through a technique called cartoon captioning (Beck, 1993). There are four parts of any cartoon: the figure doing the action or talking, what they are saying, what they are thinking, and what they are feeling. Speech can be indicated very simply with words coming out of the figure's mouth. Thoughts are placed in a "thought balloon" over the figure's head. And feelings, especially negative feelings, by something of a cloud over the figure's head.

This is illustrated below. My young nephew, Rod, just broke up with his girl and was taking it rather badly. He decided to draw a cartoon of his predicament attempting to use his new computer drawing software. Yes, the drawing wont make it into any art show or even a tabloid newspaper. But it does show that a good captioned cartoon can make a point without being artistically perfect.

LOST MY GIRLFRIEND!

The three parts of my nephew's cartoon are dramatically clear. He is shown reaching his arms out, presumably to his girl who has just left. He is crying out, "Don't leave me!" He is feeling very sad over all of this. And he is thinking "Everyone must like me."

In the dramas of our lives, it is the thought balloon that merits attention. Everyone breaks up from time to time. Some people get very upset, whereas others take it in stride. One reason why some people take such stressors badly is what happens in their thought balloons, what they say to themselves, their beliefs and expectations.

Rod's cartoon is unusually clear. However, many people confuse thoughts and feelings, as illustrated below:

> **Incorrect**: *"I feel people don't like me. My stressful thought is that 'I'm depressed.'"*
> ✓ **Correct**: *"I think people don't like me. That's my stressful thought. I feel depressed."*

> **Incorrect**: *"I feel everyone has it against me. I want to fight back. I think about being angry.*
> ✓ **Correct**: *"I think everyone has it against me. I want to fight back. I feel angry."*

There is a good reason why psychologists want us to be clear about what feelings and thoughts are. It is very difficult to directly turn off or change a feeling. When depressed, you generally can't push some internal button and become undepressed. It is far easier to change a thought than change a feeling. And feelings often come from the thoughts we have. So if we change our anxious, depressed, or angry thoughts, eventually feelings follow.

Here are two hints for keeping feelings and thoughts clear.:

1. Feeling clouds usually include such emotions as:
   - I'm sad (depressed, blue, down in the dumps)
   - I'm anxious (nervous, afraid, jittery, apprehensive)
   - Im angry (irritated, frustrated, mad, annoyed)
   - I'm happy (This goes in your feeling cloud)
2. In your thought balloon put a belief or expectation relevant to the situation. The belief or expectation should in some way contribute to or aggravate the negative feelings you have noted.

CHAPTER 19 EXERCISES

1. Create your own "soap opera" drama of exaggerations.

Soap operas are TV dramas notorious for their exaggerations. The characters routinely overreact. A lost love is experienced as the end of the world. A problem at work becomes as serious as an international crisis. In this exercise, think of a stress situation involving you or someone you know. Create a cartoon of it, including thoughts and feelings. Now, turn it into a soap opera. Exaggerate the stressful thoughts so they are clearly distorted according to the criteria in the book. What feelings would go with this exaggerated soap opera version?

2. Create your own cartoon.

Think of a recent stress situation or event. For this to work the situation needs to be specific, one where you can identify WHO was there, WHAT was done and said, WHERE you were, and WHEN it happened. In your cartoon, indicate:

- What you were doing (or what was happening)
- What you said, if anything
- What you were thinking - your beliefs and expectations
- Your negative feelings - probably some variation of sadness, anxiety, or anger.

CARTOON ABOUT SOMEONE I KNOW

CHAPTER 20
THE BIG 3 BLOCKBUSTER DISTORTIONS

Events don't automatically cause distress. Two people can react quite differently to the same stressful event. Sometimes the source of stress can be traced to a simple mistaken perception or a misunderstanding. For example

> *Last night I was frightened silly by the sound of someone in the basement – until I realized it was a cat, a burglar.*

> *I was really upset that my boss was going to fire me until I found out she was actually going to give me a raise.*

> *When my boyfriend frowned at me, I thought he didn't like my hair style. Then he explained the reason – an upset stomach.*

However, our concerns are not with everyday mistakes or misunderstandings that can be cleared up with a simple question or two. Our focus is on more subtle and persistent ways we aggravate the impact of life's stressors through our thoughts.

Distorted vs. Realistic Thoughts

Our thoughts, specifically our beliefs and expectations, are often the deciding factor in creating or setting up stress. Two psychologists, Albert Ellis and Aaron Beck, are famous for clarifying the toxic ingredient in thoughts, just what makes some beliefs and expectations more stress producing than others. Put simply, **distorted thoughts** are potentially stress-producing. **Realistic thoughts** are more likely to be associated with less stress. Here's a quick test to determine if your thought is distorted: Ask if it is:

1. Contrary to what the facts are
2. Illogical or doesn't make good sense, and
3. A Waste of time to think (why even think it if it doesn't get you anywhere?)

Here are some examples:

I must be perfect in everything I do, like my dad. I just can't accept myself if I am anything less.

- *This can't possibly be factual.* No one has ever been completely perfect.
- *This is illogical.* No one can be perfect at absolutely everything. Sometimes one has to compromise and set up priorities.
- *This is a waste of time.* You waste time trying to be perfect at things that don't particularly matter. Devote your efforts to what is really important.

I can't stand being alone! I can't go on living without a boyfriend. I must have love to survive! I'm so lonely I can't bear it any more.

- *Probably not factual.* How do you know for sure you can't live being alone? Not proven.
- *Illogical.* Many people live alone. It doesn't make sense to think that you are somehow different than the rest of the world.
- *Wasted thinking.* This complaining isn't getting you anywhere.

Learning to Distance Yourself from Stress

In this chapter we will consider one way of distancing ourselves from stress. Often stress feels serious because we are so "caught up" in it. We are so stuck in our problems that we can't see things objectively. We get carried away by stressful emotions like anger, fear, anxiety, and depression. Stress becomes like a tunnel, and we have climbed so deep into it that we can't see out.

Distancing yourself from stress involves standing back and taking perspective. It involves recognizing when our thinking may be distorted, that is, not factual, illogical, and simply a waste of time. Two powerful tricks for doing this involve labeling and humor. When we put a label our problem or our negative thinking, we automatically have to stand back a bit. When we laugh at our problems, we take one step toward defusing them.

I remember a silly cartoon of a frustrated young man standing with his nose and face pressed against a very high brick wall. The caption read something like "Damn! I'm lost! There's no where to go! I'm trapped!" The only reason he felt trapped was that his face was so tightly stuck against the wall that he couldn't see anything but bricks. If he simply took a step back, he would see all sorts of paths, walks, parks, trees around him. Indeed, we could trick him to do this by giving him a poster that reads "THIS IS A WALL, NOT A BOX." and asking him to glue it to the wall. He would have to stand back in order to paste the label on the wall. Perhaps he would recognize the absurdity of the label, and chuckle. Then he might see that we was not so trapped.

We will try a distancing tool that also uses the power of humor. We will label our stress-creating distortions as if they were silly B Movies.

The Big 3 (B Movie) Blockbuster Distortions

Let's have a little fun with a rather complicated topic. Psychologists and psychiatrists have devoted much effort to inventing lists of types of distorted thinking. These lists have grown over the years and some are now dozens of items long. Therapists often they give their lists to clients to help them evaluate their thoughts. This process can be a bit intimidating. Imagine going through a 24-item checklist every time you feel stressed!

Here's a different approach. We can consider our needlessly stressful lives as movies (perhaps "B movies"). Reviewers might observe our personal dramas and give them "two thumbs down" for being "not factual," "illogical," or simply a "waste."

Movies can be organized into various types or "genres," for example, love stories, adventure, and fantasy. Similarly, there are at least three genres of internal stressful dramas in the multiplex theaters of our lives. They are listed on the following page as three series of B movies in "The Distorted Thoughts Film Festival."

DISTORTED THOUGHTS FILM FESTIVAL

The Desperate Desire Series
The Foolish Frustration Series
The Horrible Helplessness Series

Each movie series is a type of distorted thinking. Each is a category of "stress movie" featuring how we live parts of our lives.

The Desperate Desire Series

This is the unrealistic and exaggerated feeling that you absolutely, positively MUST have something in order to be happy, go on living, be successful, and so on. Desperate Desires also include Exaggerated Expectations and Bloated Beliefs. Examples of sensible alternatives to Desperate Desires include:

"It would be nice if I could be rich, but not a desperate necessity."
"I am looking for a wife, but not frantically seeking one."
"Of course, it would be desirable if I received a raise."

Examples of Desperate Desire movies include:

1. **"Musts, oughts, and shoulds."** Turning simple honest desires and wants into absolute musts, oughts, and shoulds. "I must be a success." (Rather than "It sure would be nice to be successful, but that may or may not happen.") Or: "I should be more likable (hard-working, relaxed, rich, religious, etc")." (Rather than "I would like to be more likable.")

2. **Special privilege**. Acting as if you have a special privilege or entitlement because you are somehow more important or deserving than others. "People should always treat me nicely." "I should get what I want." "I truly deserve and must get favorable treatment."

3. **Childhood fantasy**. Assuming (as children may do) that everything should go your way. "Everyone should be nice and love each other." "Problems should have happy endings." "We should all get what we want in life."

4. **Needless perfectionism**. Picking an unfairly high standard for yourself and others, even though practically no one has ever been able to achieve it. "I should never do dumb things." "I have to be better than others."

5. **Desperate need for love and caring**. Thinking that your need for love and caring are so important (or strong) that no one can or will ever meet them. "The kind of love I need no one can provide." "I am nothing without friends or lovers."

The Foolish Frustration Series

Here the distorted thought is that a Desperate Desire isn't going to be, or has not been, met – and that is absolutely terrible, the end of the world, rather than just a frustration or disappointment. Realistic examples of alternatives include:

"Sure, I will be disappointed if I don't get an A. But that will not be the end of the world."
"I'll be irritated if he stands me up again, but I'll deal with it."
"I would like to get out of the hospital in a week, and will feel blue if I have to stay longer. But worse things could happen."

Some Foolish Frustration B movies include:

6. **Catastrophizing.** Turning simple frustrations, irritations, and disappointments into unbearable disasters and catastrophes. "I didn't get that raise (good grade, date, etc.); therefore it is the end of the world for me." "Things didn't turn out like I wanted; this is a disaster."

7. **Preoccupation on regretting the past.** Focusing on past wrongs, frustrations, and mistakes, rather than what you have or can do now. "So many things have gone wrong in my life." or "The past is filled with frustration."

8. **Negative fortune telling.** Consistently predicting the future negatively, typically thinking that things will only get worse. "I'll fail that exam or won't get the job." "I will never be really contented."

9. **Negative spin.** Arbitrarily and pessimistically putting a negative interpretation on events, even though they may be neutral or positive. "This is not what I really want." "I always look at the dark side of things."

The Horrible Helplessness Series

If a Desperate Desire isn't met, leaving you feeling Foolishly Frustrated, what could be worse? Unrealistically believing there is absolutely nothing you can do about this predicament. Then you are stuck in the rut of Horrible Helplessness. Here are some realistic alternatives:

"I'm not sure what to do about this problem. I'll brainstorm some possibilities."
"Getting the flat tire was just bad luck. It can be fixed."
"Sometimes it seems like others just ignore me. I'll have to be more assertive."

Here are some types of helpless thinking:

10. **Hyper-neediness.** Believing you can't cope by yourself and need much help from others. "I just deal with things by myself." "I always need help on important problems."

11. **Fatalism.** Believing that the uncontrollable powers of fate, your "genes," or even the Divine Supreme Being, determine the present, and that there is little we can do about it. "No use in trying to make thinks better; it's all been fated to happen this way." "It's my lot in life (my social background, genes, family) to have these problems, and there's not much I can do to change that."

12. **Imperfections = unlovability.** Feeling that you are basically defective and flawed, making you unlovable to others if they find out. "If people knew what I am really like, they would never like me." "I have flaws that will always keep people from accepting me."

13. **Unrealistic isolation.** Feeling that you are isolated from the rest of the world, different from other people, and are not, or cannot be part of any group or community. This terrible fact prevents you from doing anything about your frustrations. "I just don't belong." "I'm different from others."

14. **Needless self-blaming.** Needlessly blaming yourself for negative events, and failing to see that some events have other, complex causes. "The only reason my marriage ended is because I failed." "I broke my leg because God is punishing me."

15.   **Needless other-blaming.** Looking for someone else to blame when things don't go right. "My husband is to blame for the way I feel," or "Mother caused my problems."

16.   **Task exaggeration.** Treating simple barriers or challenges as overwhelming or insurmountable. "I don't break a problem down into manageable parts. I see the whole thing as overwhelming. If I can't immediately solve it all, why try?"

CHAPTER 20 EXERCISES

---

1. Another Person's Thinking

It can be easier to identify distorted thinking in others than in oneself. For this exercise, think of a situation where you observed distorted thinking. Describe the specifics, the WHEN, WHAT, WHERE, and WHO.

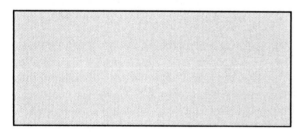

1.   What type of distorted thinking is illustrated? Desperate Desire? Foolish Frustration? Horrible Helplessness? Then identify the specific type of distorted thinking you observed

2.   Describe how this thinking is distorted. Explain which of the following are represented:

   ·   Probably not factual.
   ·   Illogical.
   ·   Wasted thinking.

2. Your Own Thinking

Think of a situation in which you had some distorted thoughts. First, describe the situation in detail

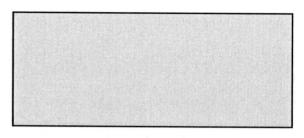

What type of distorted thinking is illustrated? Desperate Desires? Foolish Frustration? Horrible Helplessness?

Then identify the specific type of distorted thinking you observed

   ·   Probably not factual.
   ·   Illogical.
   ·   Wasted thinking.

3. Is it a B movie or a Classic?

After considering the types of distorted thinking in this chapter, one student had the following observation:

   I think I have some of these distortions, but I'm not under stress. In fact, I think some of these types of thinking help motivate me to deal with stress and do my best. I want to be my best all the time, and believe I should be this way. I do expect things will work out fine even though I think this way. If not, I guess that's just fate.

Does this thinking reflect Needless Perfectionism, Childhood Fantasy, Musts / Shoulds / Oughts, and Fatalism? Are these always negative and stress-creating lines of thinking? When are they most likely to be destructive?

CHAPTER 21
CHANGING YOUR STRESSFUL THINKING

Distorted stressful thoughts have a way of lingering. You may know very well that you make things worse by catastrophizing, overpersonalizing, or thinking in a perfectionistic way. Simply having this understanding may not be enough.

Changing stressful thinking habits can be like changing any habit. It takes time and practice. I recommend trying may tools again and again. Eventually you may find which fit you best and use them automatically at the first sign of stressful thinking.

The fist step is to identify which of your beliefs and expectations are creating stress. Complete the "thought balloon" exercise in Chapter 19. Select a type of distorted thinking from Chapter 20

Then **do a reality check**. That is, challenge the distortion. Think it through. Decide on a replacement thought that is more realistic. However, reality checking is not a quick fix. It is a skill, like swimming or dancing. You have to practice over and over and over before it begins to sink in. Important skills involve creating real changes in the brain, and this doesn't happen overnight.

The goal of this chapter is to give you extensive practice in making reality checks. We make this job a little easier by considering the process of reality checking from various perspectives.

Reality Checking Tools

This chapter offers four types of reality-checking you might consider. The **basic smell test** is the simplest and fastest check. You simply examine a thought and ask "Hey, is this really true?" It's like going to a market, picking up a piece of fish, sniffing it, and asking "Hey, is this fish OK??" The **quick check** is something like checking yourself in the mirror in the morning to see if your hair, tie, lipstick, teeth, etc. are OK. You check a specific idea of feeling to see if it passes the reality test. More involved is the process of **self-analysis**. Here you set some time aside to do some honest thinking as part of your reality check. The **positive alternative** involves deliberately considering realistically hopeful and optimistic lines of thought. Browse through this library. Try those which seem to catch your interest. See which work for you.

The Basic Smell Test

Do this one first. Simply look at what you are thinking. Can you find a thought that is obviously distorted? Obviously out of touch with the facts? An unprovable guess? Just plain silly and illogical? A pointless waste of time? If so the thought doesn't pass the "basic smell test." Toss it out.

The Quick Check

1. **Are you using words that are vague, global, and judgmental?** "I am a complete failure." Just what is a complete failure? "I got an F on my first exam." "She is evil." Define evil. "She didn't return my call."

2. **Are you unfairly evaluating persons rather than behaviors?** "I failed as a person." vs. "I failed the midterm." "I am a terrible husband." vs. "I made a mistake."

3. **Are you distinguishing unrealistic desires and expectations from simple preferences?** "I feel like I must get that promotion, or I could never live with myself." vs. "I want a promotion."

4. **Are you distinguishing certainties from possibilities?** "I will get nervous during the interview and forget everything." vs. "I will probably get a bit nervous during the interview, but it is very unlikely I will forget everything."

5. **Is your thinking needlessly rigid, one-sided, or inflexible?** "I think in all - or -nothing terms," versus "I recognize there are shades of gray." "It's this way, and there's no other way of looking at it." vs. "Maybe there are alternative perspectives I haven't considered."

6. **Are you exaggerating simple feelings, or letting one feeling color your whole world?** "Everyone is so irritating" vs. "So I'm angry; I don't have to wear a dark pair of glasses that colors and distorts the whole world according to my mood." "I'm a bit anxious over the speech I have to give; that's not good." vs. "It's normal to feel a bit nervous."

7. **Are you mind-reading?** "She looked at me. That must mean she doesn't like me." vs. "She looked at me. What does that mean?" "You're trying to analyze me. I can see it in your smile." vs. "You're smiling at me, and I don't know what you're thinking. That makes me a bit uncomfortable."

8. **Are you setting up impossible expectations?.** "I want to be perfect in everything and never give up a task." Trying to be perfect at many tasks means you have to be less than perfect at others (to have enough time to be perfect).

Self-Analysis

1. **Weigh evidence for and against a thought.** "People think that I don't know what I am talking about when I'm having a discussion." *Let's list all the times you had clear evidence that people thought you did not know what you were talking about, and all the times when you had evidence people thought you did know what you were talking about.* "Evidence for: People tell me I'm stupid; people walking away; people telling other people that they think I don't know things. I have no evidence any of this has happened. Evidence against: people continuing to talk with me, people ask me questions -- I must know something. .This happened about six times this week."

2. **Consider full chain of consequences, and evaluate.** "I didn't get the raise, and that's the end of the world." *What's the consequence of not getting the raise?* "I won't be able to fix the car or remodel the basement." *What's the consequence of that?* "My car will be less comfortable and more noisy when I drive. *What's the consequence, is that so bad?* "I'll still get places in my car, I'll still be able to entertain."

3. **Test the thought with an experiment.** "When I talk to my friends, they really don't want to talk with me and want to be somewhere else." *Let's design an experiment to test this out.* "The next 10 friends and acquaintances I start to talk to, I could suggest, 'I know you might be a bit busy, would you rather continue this later sometime?' Record when someone agrees and walks away."

4. **Examine if past worries or predictions haven't come true or are no longer important.** "I know I'll mess up this date. I'm always worrying about how things will go wrong." *Let's look at past things you have or might have worried about. Let's see which have actually come true? Which are no longer important?*

5. **Apply the same standard to everyone else.** "I am a weak person because I can't immediately calm down whenever I'm in a stressful situation." *Is it reasonable to call everyone weak when they can't immediately calm down in stressful situations? Why or why not?* "I do not have a wife; therefore I must be unlovable." *Is everyone who does not have a wife unlovable? Be fair to yourself.*

6. **Question how others might evaluate the quality of your evidence and thinking.** "I'm just no good at work." Why is that? "Yesterday I was five minutes late, last week I couldn't find my report, and today I forgot to make a phone call." *Imagine you are (name a friend you can trust). Realistically how would this person rate you if the knew these facts about your work?*

The Positive Alternative

1. **Look for mitigating circumstances.** Are you being to hard on yourself? Are there certain circumstances, people, or past events that should be taken into account?

2. **Anticipate realistic possible futures that put things in perspective.** "Yes, we've talked about this for quite some time. My employer is going out of business and I won't have a job next month." Lets stand back and think about a year, two years, even five years from now. What kinds of things might happen that would cause you to look back at today and say 'that wasn't so bad after all'? "I hope I'll be married. I certainly will have another job, hopefully one that is stable.

3. **What is the possible "silver lining" in this cloud? What possible good could come from this?** "My illness will get me to pay more attention to my health, something I need to do."

"I lost out on this interview. At least it taught me some good things about interviewing." "Sometime's it's important to learn to accept things that cannot change, and go on living." "I am learning how to forgive."

4. **Examine what might be worse, or others who might be worse off**. "I was turned down for that promotion yesterday." I understand how that might be frustrating, but it's not the worst thing that could happen. "Yes, I could have been fired, demoted, transferred out of state, put in a smaller office, or given a bad review." "Think of all of the people who have been fired from work this year."

5. **Consider what is possibly funny about this situation**. "I was at the grocery with a full cart. I turned the corner and collided into another cart. Mine turned over and spilled everything. I felt so embarrassed." Anything amusing about this situation?

Hidden Distortions: Digging up the Dirt

One distorted thought can be the tip of deeper hidden distorted thoughts. For example, a gardener may discover a strange blue wire sticking up out the lawn. She asks, "Why is that there?" Then she digs it up and discovers a child's toy that had been buried years ago. When it comes to distorted thinking, we are all gardeners. The shovel we use to uncover hidden weeds and distorted thinking is "The Why Question."

You simply note a negative thought, and ask, "Why is this important to me? So what?" Whatever answer then emerges, ask again, "Why is this important to me? So what?" When asked repeatedly, the "Why question" can unearth deeper distorted beliefs. Here's an example:

Joan criticized me at work and I got upset. Why is that important to me? Because I don't want Joan to criticize me at work, and I don't want to get upset. Why is this important to me? So what? Why don't I want Joan to criticize me at work? Actually, I don't want anyone at work to criticize me. Why is it important that people at work don't criticize you? It is important to me that I be liked by everyone. I need to be liked.

Once you have identified what appears to be a deeper and more general distortion ("I need to be liked"), you can do a reality check. There is a payoff to identifying deep and general distortions.

Imagine you are trying to teach your young child not to play in mud puddles in the street. You discover your child playing with her Barbie doll in the mud. You reply, "Please do not play with your doll in the mud, you will get its hair dirty." Then you discover your child playing with a toy car in the mud. You say, "Please do not play with your toy car in the mud. You will get it all clogged up with dirt." Once again you catch the child playing, this time with a stuffed animal in the mud. You ask yourself, "Why is this important to me? Because I don't want my child and her toys to get covered with unhealthy dirt." You then explain to the child, "Please do not play in the mud. Playing in the mud is dirty and can make you sick."

In this example, your first confronted specific problems, just as one might confront specific distorted thoughts. You then decided to address the more general problem, dirt. This is similar to confronting a more general distorted belief. The payoff of confronting a general problem is that you automatically deal with all specific types of this problem – playing in the dirty mud includes everything, playing with dolls, toy cars, stuffed animals, food, makeup, boats, etc.

Here are some example of deep general distortions and specific examples. Remember, we unearth deep general distortions by asking the "Why?" question:

Specific Distorted Thoughts. I must be perfect at my job. I must be the perfect husband. I must have the perfect car. Why is this important to me?
Deep General Distortion: I must be perfect in all things in order to accept myself.

Specific Distorted Thoughts: My friends lie to me. My coworkers make up stories. I can't believe my kids anymore. Why is this important to me?
Deep General Distortion: I want people always to tell the truth. You can't trust anyone.

CHAPTER 21 EXERCISES

1. Favorite distortions.

What are your three favorite types of distorted thinking from the previous chapter? Challenge and replace each in the space below.

2. Challenging Distorted Thinking Examples

Below are some examples of distorted thinking. For each, describe

· The type of distortion
· How you might challenge it effectively

1. Jim is a college student who just interviewed for a part-time job at the school cafeteria. He didn't get it. Here's his worry: "I'm just a no good slub. Nobody wants me."

   · The type of distortion

   · How you might challenge it effectively

2. Freeda has just discovered a problem. She promised her mosque that she would help in their weekend cleaning project. She forgot and didn't show up. Instead, she went to the zoo. "I'm just a terrible person. How could I possibly do such a thing? I've disappointed and hurt so many people. Unforgivable!"

   · The type of distortion

   · How you might challenge it effectively

3. Josh has had his eyes on a young classmate, Gretchen. Finally he musters up the courage to ask her out for a coffee. She says she's too busy. "I feel terrible! I'm so depressed. Women just don't like me. What's wrong with me?"

   · The type of distortion

   · How you might challenge it effectively

4. Birttany has been studying her Bible very hard for church school. She has been doing a lot of thinking about her life and wonders if some changes might me in order. "I must love everyone all of the time. I must love people for who they are, accept them 'as is,' without judgement." But how can I love people I don't know? And honestly, I just don't like some people, like murderers.

- The type of distortion

- How you might challenge it effectively

5. Bud was walking down the sidewalk with his books and a full cup of Starbuck's coffee. A group of four teens were walking in his direction. They were completely absorbed in laughing and talking about something they saw on TV. As they passed, one teen gently bumped Bud's left arm, causing him to spill his coffee all over his new Nike shoes. Bud stopped, looked down to assess the damage, and realized they would have to be cleaned. When he looked up, the teens were several feet away, still laughing and talking. "People should always think about how their actions might affect others. Everyone is so damn inconsiderate!" He spend the rest of the day thinking about this.

- The type of distortion

- How you might challenge it effectively

6. Shelah has to give a talk in class. She is very nervous. "I will forget everything and everyone will think that I did not prepare or that I'm stupid or on drugs."

- The type of distortion

- How you might challenge it effectively

7. George has a drinking problem. He has been drinking every day and night. Finally, he had enough and decided to stop. He went to the library instead to study for class. There he met some of his drinking buddies who invited him out for a drink. He went along, and felt very very guilty. "Nothing's ever going to change. I just don't have what it takes to resist what my friends want."

- The type of distortion

- How you might challenge it effectively

3. Your distorted thinking.

Think of a recent stressful situation made worse by distorted thinking. What type of thinking was it? How would you challenge and replace it?

CHAPTER 22
WORRY? STOP! HA! BE MINDFUL!

Worry can be a bad habit, like biting nails. Psychologists say that bad habits often arise because they are rewarded. Your dog Fido may be banned from jumping on the sofa. However, he frequently does this because as a pup he received lavish praise while playing on the sofa. One way of breaking bad habits is to take away the reward. But what is the reward for worrying? Perhaps the unrealistic fantasy that you might eventually discover "the answer," or that you should not waste time avoiding a problem. Maybe you feel "good and productive" when worrying. What distorted thoughts can you identify for continuing to worry?

Worry Sessions

One way of teaching Fido not to hop and play on the sofa is to give him his own playbed, perhaps next to the sofa. This way you can praise and reward hi whenever he hops onto his playbed. You have removed the reward for sitting on the sofa.

Thomas Borkovec (Borkovec, 1985; Borkovec, Wilkinson, Folensbee, & Lerman, 1983) has developed a similar exercise for dealing with worry. First you identify the places you are most likely to worry. Be specific. Do you worry on the subway, during lunch, while watching TV?

Then set aside a special half-hour time every day reserved just for intensive worry. You can't worry any other time of the day, just during this worry period. Whenever you catch yourself wanting to worry, simply say "later" and go on with your work.

Worry ➜ Stop! Ha! Snap!

Another strategy thought stopping (Cautela & Wisocki, 1977), focuses on the consequences of worry. Here is a summary of my version (Smith, 2002). When Fido jumps on the sofa, you might firmly order, "Off!" This negative consequence may be enough to stop his habit. In thought stopping one deliberately follows worry with a simple aversive consequence, snapping a rubber band.

Session 1

First, place a rubber band on your wrist.
Make a list of negative worries, for example:

"I must be perfect."
"Nobody likes me."
"I am just a weakling."
"Things are going to get really really bad."

Next pick one negative thought from this list, for example:

"I must be perfect."
"Everything I do must be just right."

Do a reality check of this thought, using Chapters 24 and 25. It is important for you to accept that this thought is actually distorted. For example, you might decide:

"It is silly to think I must be perfect all the time. I need a little slack!" " It's good to do my best at things that matter, but no one has the energy to do this for everything. Get some perspective!."

Now relax, perhaps by practicing one of the relaxation exercises in this book. Then start worrying. Think the thought you have just targeted. And when you begin thinking this thought, yell "STOP!" While snapping your rubber band. As you can imagine, this is a bit disruptive. That's the point. You disrupt and interrupt the worry.
Here's an alternative. Instead of yelling STOP!, laugh out loud for a full 60 seconds. Then wait and relax. Once the thought comes back, yell and snap again. Do for 15 minutes.

Session 2

This time you repeat the process. Relax. However, when any negative worry comes to mind, simply say the word STOP! or gently laugh. Snap the rubber band as before. Do for 15 minutes.

Session 3

Relax again. And when a worry comes to mind think STOP! or laugh quietly in your mind. Snap the rubber band again.

Do for 15 minutes.

This variation is very portable. You can do it on the bus, while shopping, and even when you are stuck in traffic. It can be summarized:

RELAX - WORRY ➡-STOP! (HA!) - SNAP

Worry ➡ Relax

Consider the approaches to relaxation taught in this text. Once you have mastered one or more approaches, select a quick 2-minute mini-relaxation based on what you have learned. For example, if you enjoy breathing exercises, you might breathe out through your lips as your mini-relaxation.

Then, set aside one hour during your day in which you actually follow every instance of worry with a mini-relaxation. Begin the day with a full relaxation sequence.

The Eye Movement Exercise

Smyth (1996) has devised a clever way of getting your mind off your worries. His eye movement exercise simply involves deliberately shifting your eyes back and forth when you catch yourself engaging in a identified worry. It seems to be especially useful for worrisome thoughts that do not evoke high levels of anxiety. Here are the steps.

1. Identify a thought, image, or worry you want to manage. For example, "Everyone is looking at me." Or "I did such a poor job at school."
2. What's your general stress level when the thought starts? On a scale from 0 (total relaxation) to 10 (maximum stress), how do you feel now.
3. If your stress level is elevated (5 or 6), sit or stand still. Pick two focus points, one to your left and one to your right. You might pick corners of a room, or two opposing windows. Then quickly move your eyes back and fourth from one focal point to another, twenty to twenty-five times.
4. When finished, rate your stress level again.

It is fine to repeat this exercise after ten minutes, or do it with your eyes closed (especially in a room with other people who might notice your shifty-eyes!). Try it after a mini-relaxation.

Worry Mindfully

Mindfulness meditation (Chapter 11) offers a different strategy for dealing with worry. In mindfulness meditation, you calmly accept and attend to whatever comes your way. You do not think about anything you notice. You do not try to avoid, cling, evaluate as desired or undesired. You simply attend. For example, if you were to mindfully meditate on a street, you would not think about the street (or your day, your frustrations, etc.). You notice truck. Quietly note the truck, and continue waiting and attending, until you notice something else, perhaps a red car. And you note the red car and go on attending. Mindfulness meditation is simply noting and attending, without dwelling on or thinking about anything.

Worry can easily intrude into a mindfulness meditation. When this happens, you treat the intrusion as you would treat any other stimulus, like a barking dog or honking car. Simply note it ("Oh, another worry about my job. Back to attending.") Let go. Continue attending.

Through such mindful attending one gradually deprives worrisome thoughts of their "charge" or energy. They become simple, neutral distractions that come and go, like barking dogs in the distance.

CHAPTER 22 EXERCISES

1. Why worry?

What distorted thoughts do you have that may contribute to continued worry?

2. Trying Out Worry-Stopping Strategies

This week try out each of the three worry strategies suggested in this chapter:

Worry Session

STOP! HA!

Mindfulness

Try no more than one strategy each day. Then rate how well each worked for you.

CHAPTER 23
THE 3 DEEP QUESTIONS

Three categories of distorted thinking can create stress: Desperate Desire, Foolish Frustration, and Horrible Helplessness (see Chapter 20). We may desperately desire things that are unrealistic or impossible, such as

I want to be perfect in all things.
I want to be loved by everyone.

We may exaggerate the frustration of not getting we want:

Not getting what I want is the end of the world.
This is a terrible catastrophe.

We may feel utterly and unrealistically helpless.

I guess I am just fated to be unhappy. There's nothing I can do about it.
Everyone's out to get me. There's no way I can succeed when no one wants to help

We conclude Part IV of this book, Thinking Realistically, with three philosophical questions that can play an important role in reducing stress. These deep questions are profound and positive versions of our three types of distorted thinking.

QUESTION 1
What is Truly Important in Your Life?
Direction and Purpose

All desperate desires can be seen as misplaced or confused priorities. Consider a person who says "I

desperately want to be perfect in all things." Is this really what's most important to you? More important than health, love, or happiness? Surely there times where you would be willing to give up a chance at winning in order to achieve some higher goal. A student may want to earn an A in every class, but have to take a few weeks off to care for a sick mother. He accepts a lower grade in order to offer help.

We can all think of instances that force us to put our everyday wants and goals in perspective. We pause and consider the question, what is the most important thing in life? What trumps every other goal? Happiness? Health? Family? Friends? One's country? God?

QUESTION 2
What's it Worth?
Meaningful Sacrifice, Delayed Gratification

What frustrations can you accept when working toward your most important goal? What immediate satisfactions are you willing to put off and delay? Your answer to the first question puts all frustrations into perspective.

QUESTION 3
Positive Choices
What are you going to Do about It?

In Chapter 20, we defined Horrible Helplessness as the belief that one is helpless, perhaps because of blaming oneself and others, feeling defective or imperfect, or simply because of bad fate or genes.

When considering the three Deep Questions, Horrible Helplessness is not an option. If you have picked a goal or concern that is truly of commanding importance, then you have committed yourself to accept the temporary frustrations of taking risks, exploring, and trying. You have committed yourself to try, learn from setbacks, and try again. You have a reason to act, even though success is not assured. We can summarize the relationship between distorted and deep thinking like this:

DISTORTED THINKING

- **Desperate Desire**

- **Foolish Frustration**

- **Horrible Helplessness**

DEEP THINKING

- **Direction and Purpose**

- **Meaningful Sacrifice Delayed Gratification**

- **Positive Choices**

PART V
BASIC APPLICATIONS

CHAPTER 24
DESENSITIZATION

Julia is only 9 years old and is very afraid of the water. When the rest of her family goes swimming, she screams and complains, and wants to stay home. One Summer, the family decided to spend a month at a cabin. A few hundred feet away was a small lake, perfect for swimming. On the first day, the entire family had a picnic on the beach, a few dozen feet from the lake. This was relaxing and fun. Julia at first felt a little nervous, but quickly adjusted. The next day the family built sand castles on the beach, just a few feet from the lake. Again, Julia was initially a little uptight, but she quickly got involved in play and forgot about the water. On the third day, the family again built castles in the sand, this time surrounding them with a moat. To fill the moat with water, a small trench had to be dug a few feet to the lake. This made Julia a bit uncomfortable, but she recovered. On the fourth day the family sat in a shallow part of the pond and splashed each other with water. The next day they waded in a few more feet, and tossed the beach ball around. Eventually, the entire family, including Julia, was playing and swimming.

Julia overcame her fear of water through a simple and sensible process called desensitization. We desensitize to a fear by first getting very relaxed (through a relaxation exercise), and then approaching a very easy and nonthreatening version of the fear. Once we can do this without anxiety, we increase the stakes, and repeat the process, this time on a slightly more threatening version. When we can confront this version without getting upset, we introduce a slightly more serious variation of the stressor. Eventually, we condition ourselves to remain relaxed even when doing the thing that initially made us upset.

Learning to Relax

First, you must master an approach to relaxation. Do not continue until you can achieve the relaxation response, and feel deeply at ease and relaxed, in a relatively short period of time. You will have to use your quick relaxation procedure again and again in desensitization, otherwise it won't work.

Building a Hierarchy

First, select a topic, a situation or activity that creates so much anxiety or distress that you either avoid it or have difficulty engaging in it. Then, create ten versions of your topic, ranging from very easy to very challenging. In your "Top Ten List," item number 1 should evoke very little or no tension. If it creates tension, then it is too severe and perhaps should be placed higher on your hierarchy. Item number 10 should be the most severe version of your selected theme. It should create sufficient distress that you almost certainly avoid it or have difficulty when confronting it. The remaining items, 2-9, should be increasingly severe.

Make sure your items are realistic, under your control, and not risk your health or well-being. So, for this exercise, avoid topics like "racing my car on the streets," "lighting a huge firecracker indoors," "approaching a live bear in the wild," or "swimming alone in a quarry at night." Here is a simple hierarchy for asking for a raise.

The Boss on my Mind

10.   *Meeting with my boss alone and asking for a raise.*
9.   *Phoning my boss and asking for a raise.*
8.   *Meeting with my boss to review my performance.*
7.   *Writing an e-mail to my boss informing him that the office workers would like a new water cooler.*
6.   *Having lunch with my boss and other coworkers*
5.   *Riding home with my boss on the subway.*
4.   *Meeting my boss unexpectedly in the grocery store.*
3.   *Talking about my boss to coworkers at work*
2.   *Talking about my boss to my family at home.*
1.   *Looking at a photo of my boss on my work desk.*

This was a very simple hierarchy of loosely related events. You may want each item in a hierarchy to reflect an actual step you are taking, with each step brining you close to a situation or event that creates anxiety. We see this in the following hierarchy for fear of flying. Note that this fear is not based on any fact, but it prevents the person from flying.

Fear of Flying

10.   *I am safely in the airplane, and we hit a little turbulence.*
9.   *I am safely n the airplane, and I can see the ground far below.*
8.   *We are taking off.*
7.   *I am sitting in the plane waiting to take off.*
6.   *I am boarding the plane*
5.   *I am waiting at the airport for the plane to arrive.*
4.   *I am being checked at the airport.*
3.   *I am arriving at the airport in the bus.*
2.   *I am driving to the bus that goes to the airport.*
1.   *I am packing my gear for the flight today.*

Creating Detailed Fantasies of each Hierarchy Item

Once you have created your hierarchy, the next step is to create a detailed description of each item. Each description should be as vivid and as realistic as possible. Include Who is there, When it is happening, Where it is happening, and What is happening. In addition, describe the thoughts and feelings you have. Here is an example of item No.1 for Fear of Flying:

THEME: Fear of Flying
ITEM NO.1: Packing my gear for the flight today

Today I take my first flight in over five years. It has me really uptight! I've put off packing until the last moment, but now it has to be done. I think about what size of bag I will need. Will they want to open the bag? I shouldn't carry on a bag that is too big. And I have to avoid anything that looks sharp, otherwise the metal detector will go off. I feel myself starting to sweat as I think about the flight and what I will have to do to get ready. What if they turn me away? What if the flight is cancelled? What if they lose my luggage? I better take along stuff that isn't too valuable. And I don't want anyone taking my bag by mistake, so I'll make sure my bag is clearly identified. It should have a lock so no one gets in. I slowly put my shirts and pants into the bag, along with toothpaste. What if the drop in air pressure causes my toothpaste to burst? I better put it in a bag. Will I have enough time to get to the plane and get on?

Doing Desensitization

Once you have your ten detailed descriptions, you are ready to begin desensitization. Here's the process:

1. Select the lowest hierarchy item. Practice your preferred relaxation technique until you are deeply relaxed.
2. Begin fantasizing the item you have selected. You may read what you have in your description, adding vivid details as they come to mind. Or you can imagine you are describing the item to a friend, including as much detail as possible. **The instant you experience the slightest anxiety, STOP. Begin your relaxation exercise again until you are relaxed. Then start over with the same item**. Keep repeating this cycle: fantasizing or describing the item – relaxing – fantasizing or describing the item – relaxing until you are able to fantasize or describe every detail. When you can do this and your level of anxiety is no more than half what it was initially, you're done with that item. Next session, continue with Item No. 2 on your hierarchy.

In summary, you want to be able to stay with your hierarchy item and experience at least a 50 percent reduction in anxiety. If you get stuck at an item (and have trouble getting to the 50 percept point), try backing up and repeating an earlier item. Or create and insert a new item that is slightly easier than the item that is causing trouble.

CHAPTER 23 EXERCISES

1. **What's wrong with this hierarchy? Making a desensitization hierarchy is more difficult that it may seem. The following hierarchy has many mistakes. Can you find them?**

THEME: Going to the dentist to have my teeth worked on

#10   Having the dentist replace an entire tooth.
#9 Breaking my arm.
#8 Having to stay home a week because of stomach flu.
#7 Having a tooth pulled.
#6 The dentist telling he has to pull a tooth.
#5 Talking to my minister about something I did wrong.
#4 Having to stay overnight with my girl's mother.
#3 Having my teeth cleaned.
#2 Introducing myself to a person I want to meet at a party.
#1 I am walking home thinking about the dentist

2   Your Desensitization Hierarchy

Think of a desensitization theme that fits your life. Then
create a 10-item hierarchy.

THEME:

#10

#9

#8

#7

#6

#5

#4

#3

#2

#1

3. Creating Hierarchy Descriptions

First assemble ten blank cards (or sheets of paper) Then create a detailed description for each item on your hierarchy, one per card (or sheet). Remember: (1) Keep it realistic (you are not writing a fantastic horror script! (2) Make it very very vivid, including specific and concrete details

CHAPTER 25
RELAPSE PREVENTION

Often the tools of stress management are most effective when one plans ahead. One very useful way of planning ahead involves considering the possibilities of setback and failure. This is the idea underlying relapse prevention.

Marlatt and Gordon (1984) describe a relapse as a special type of stressor, one in which your attempted coping efforts unexpectedly do not work and you face failure and setback. You may forget your lines while giving a lecture. You may get a grade of D instead of the expected A in a course. Perhaps your boss rejects your request for a modest raise.

Such unexpected failures or setbacks can lead to stress-producing distorted thinking. You may believe you are helpless, or have to worry constantly to solve your problems.

Relapse prevention treats the possibility of failure and setback as a stressor in itself. It is a way of insuring yourself against failure or setback. You anticipate possible setbacks, and develop "Plan Bs" or alternative backup coping strategies. There are two types of relapse strategies: comebacks and fallbacks.

Comeback Strategies

A comeback strategy is a very simple alternative plan, one you put into effect once it becomes clear your plans are not working. For example:

Tomorrow I will take my defective radio back to the store and ask for my money back. Even though I don't have the receipt, I bought the radio yesterday and know the clerk. If I chicken out and don't go to the store, my backup plan is to practice relaxation for half an hour and go "I plan to assertively return this piece of defective merchandise tomorrow and ask for my money back. If I get cold feet and 'forget,' I will practice my relaxation exercise and try again the next day. That will give me a chance to practice my relapse prevention skills.

Fallback Strategies

What do you do when coping and comeback don't work? A fallback strategy is your coping option of last resort, one you use when all else fails. A fallback strategy is something like the safety net circus performers use when swing high over the crowd. If the rope breaks, at least they will be caught by the net. A fallback strategy is like the extra stash of cash you may have tucked away for a rainy day. Sometimes the best fallback strategies are positive, realistic, and supportive things we say to yourselves, such as (Meichenbaum, 1985; Smith, 1993a):

Well, life goes on.
Everyone makes mistakes.
I still love myself (or have a loving family) in spite of my problems.
Lets look at things in perspective. Life is too short to make too much of this problem.
I'll treat this as water under the bridge.
Maybe I'll learn somehow from this.

Phases of Stress

One effective way of anticipating relapse is to divide an upcoming stress event into stages. I find it useful to think of four phases: pre-stress, onset-stress, mid-stress, and post-stress. Then, consider comeback and fallback strategies for each. The pre-stress refers to the time before a stress event. Onset-stress is the moment the event begins. Mid-stress is the actual stress event. And post-stress is the time after the event is over. For example, imagine you are about to interview for a job. Here are the phases:

Pre-stress:	*The day before the interview. You are thinking about and planning for the interview.*
Onset-stress	*You arrive at the setting of the interview, walk in the office, and shake hands with the interviewer.*
Mid-stress	*The interview starts, continues, and ends.*

Post-stress   It's over. You return home.

Preparing your Relapse Strategies

Preparing your relapse prevention strategies involves three steps:

1. Identify the four phases of your stress event.
2. Identify what might go wrong in each stress.
3. Create a comeback and fallback strategy for each. This may include specific actions or appropriate thoughts.

Meichenbaum (1985) and others provide a number of examples of comeback and fallback thoughts for each phase of stress.

Pre-Stress

"It's a good idea to practice problem-solving, regardless of the outcome."
"Most people get a little tense before a stressful encounter."
"Stress energy can actually help me do better."
"I'll do my best, and that is all I can reasonably expect of myself."
"I will just keep my mind on what I'm doing, rather than on worrying."

Onset-Stress

"Things are starting. Stress is normal."
"Stay with the plan.   Keep organized."
"Let's try a quickie relaxation. Just breathe slowly, out of the lips."
"I've thought ahead my coping and relapse plans."
"Soon this whole thing will be over."
"Most people don't notice when you get cold hands or feel nervous."

Mid-Stress

"Keep on going. I'm practicing using my coping skills.""
"Think realistically."
"Take it easy; don't try to do it all at once."
"Makes no sense to take setbacks personally."
"Remember to take a positive, problem-solving perspective."
"Let's not catastrophise."
"Don't focus on the stress, just the job."
"Relax. Use my relaxation mini-relaxation"

Post-Stress

"Let's analyze objectively what went right and where there is room for improvement"
"This is a learning opportunity."
"Remember to recognize what went right."
"No one's perfect."
"I've learned what to do differently the next time."
"Time to relax!"

CHAPTER 24 EXERCISES

1. Phases of a stressor.

Identify a stressor in your life in which relapse is possible. In the spaces below, describe pre-stress, onset-stress, mid-stress, and post-stress phases. Be as concrete and specific as possible.

PRE-STRESS
ONSET-STRESS
MID-STRESS
POST-STRESS

2. What could go wrong?

For each phase of the stressor you described on the previous page, identify one or two things that might go wrong, one or two coping failures or setbacks you might experience.   Then, think of a comeback and fallback strategy (actions / thoughts) for each.

PRE-STRESS

Relapse Possibilities   Comeback/Fallback

ONSET-STRESS

Relapse Possibilities   Comeback/Fallback

MID-STRESS

Relapse Possibilities   Comeback/Fallback

P
POST-STRESS

Relapse Possibilities   Comeback/Fallback

CHAPTER 26
ASSERTIVENESS

To be assertive is to honestly and effectively say what you want, think, and feel, while respecting the wants, thoughts, and feelings of others. Assertiveness training is a standard part of most stress management programs. It is usually contrasted with passivity, aggressiveness, and at times, passive-aggressiveness. Passive people do not say what they want, think, or feel. They keep to themselves, unheard and unrecognized. Problems are left unresolved, and wants unfulfilled.

Aggressive people may well say what's on their mind, but without respecting the wants, thoughts, and feelings of others.

Passive-aggressive people passively do not directly and effectively say what's on their minds. However, they express aggression in a variety of indirect ways, such as getting even, being dishonest, or pouting.

Examples

People often think they are assertive, when if fact they're not. We can see this in the following:

Housecleaning

Sue and Jane have lived together for months. They have agreed to divide their chores so that each would have that responsibility every other week. Sue has not done her chores for a week. Jane decides to say something.

Assertive. *Sue, I though we agreed we would split the chores of cleaning house. This week was your turn, and you've haven't vacuumed or dusted. I know this work isn't fun. But I'm frustrated and feel like I'm doing more than my share. I would feel better if we could come to an agreement we both stick to.*

Aggressive. *Sue, you are just a lazy pig.*

Passive. *Sue, you know, I wonder if we could help each other out a little more. There would be a lot less tension, you know.*

Passive-Aggressive. *Gosh, you know what's happened? I just won't have the time to clean*

the apartment next month. We're having guests over, I'm sure you won't mind if I put our junk in your bedroom.

Requesting a New Computer at Work

Jerome has been working as an accountant for over a year at a big downtown business. The policy is that anyone who has worked for over six month gets a new computer, rather than use the old common computer. Jerome is overdue. Business has been very good, and others have received their computers. He decides to talk to his supervisor.

Assertive. *When I started work, you promised I would get a new computer after six months. It has been a year, others have their new computers, and I still use the communal computer. I would like to talk about what is going on, and if I can expect a new computer.*

Aggressive. *I feel you are not honoring our contract or respecting your workers. You dont give a darn about any of us! I find it difficult to work under these conditions, and feel slighted.*

Passive. *Gosh, it's getting more and more difficult to complete all my work on the communal computer. I have to wait in line for my turn, and work doesn't get done.*

Passive-Aggressive. *Actually, I have no problem using the communal computer, even though I was promised my own new computer. I enjoy working with others. And waiting my turn gives me extra time to catch up on local gossip with my coworkers.*

Assertiveness is a Coping Option

There is a time to be assertive and a time to be nonassertive. However, it is useful to have an assertive option available in case you want to use it. In order to have this option, you need to know what to say and do, and understand the costs and benefits.

In many cases, assertive people are more likely to get what they want, enlist the cooperation and help of others, enjoy satisfying relationships, and have a higher opinion of themselves.

Passive (and passive-aggressive) people, because they keep their wants, thoughts, and feelings themselves, are more likely to be frustrated and not get what they want. They are more likely to be manipulated and injured by others. The passive person is more likely to experience stress and distorted thinking, and less likely to resolve stressful problems. As a result, he or she may have difficulties with deep relaxation exercises and not experience the benefits of relaxation states of mind in everyday life. Aggressive (and passive-aggressive) people may temporarily get what they want and feel satisfied and powerful. Others are more likely to feel resentful and not cooperative, relationships are injured, and some wants may not be fulfilled. Long-term problem-solving is not enhanced and self-serving distorted thinking may persist. Generally, the aggressive person carries an additional burden of physical and psychological tension that can interfere with both practicing a relaxation exercise and enjoying relaxation throughout work and leisure.

However, sometimes the benefits of passivity outweigh the benefits of assertiveness. If you are discussing your parking ticket and believe your police officer used and unpleasant tone of voice, perhaps it would be better to passively keep that complaint to yourself. If you are the repeated victim of a racial slur by the neighborhood bully, perhaps giving him or her a piece of your mind (and getting the anger off your chest) wouldn't be such a bad idea.

One important key to assertiveness is knowing to consider and weigh the costs and benefits of each before making a decision.

Nonverbal Behaviors

`The way you stand, the postures you assume, and your tone of voice can do much to clearly communicate assertiveness, passivity, aggressiveness, and passive-aggressiveness. For example, the assertive person stands up straight, looks you straight in the eye, speaks clearly and confidently, and uses appropriate gestures. A passive person is more likely to slouch, look aside, speak quietly, and not use gestures. An aggressive person shows hostility in posture, voice, and gesture. Make sure your nonverbal behaviors go with the assertive option you select.

CHAPTER 25 EXERCISES

1. Thoughts and beliefs

What we think and believe can lead to or get in the way of being assertive. Alberti and Emmons (1982) and Jakubowski and Lange (1978) have listed beliefs and thoughts that may be conducive to behavior that is assertive or nonassertive. Below are some of what they have suggested. Indicate which are most conducive to behavior that is:

❏ Assertive ❏ Passive ❏ Aggressive ❏ Passive-Aggressive

Then explain why.

1.   You have the right to dignity and self-respect
      ❏ Assertive ❏ Passive ❏ Aggressive ❏ Passive-Aggressive

2.   If you express your anger indirectly, others will get your point.
      ❏ Assertive ❏ Passive ❏ Aggressive ❏ Passive-Aggressive

3.   It is cool not to say what you want, but cause trouble for others who cause problems.
      ❏ Assertive ❏ Passive ❏ Aggressive ❏ Passive-Aggressive

4.   You must have the approval of others.
      ❏ Assertive ❏ Passive ❏ Aggressive ❏ Passive-Aggressive

5.   The world is a dangerous, hostile place where one always has to be on guard.
      ❏ Assertive ❏ Passive ❏ Aggressive ❏ Passive-Aggressive

6.   It is better to pretend that things are OK, and hurt the other person indirectly.
      ❏ Assertive ❏ Passive ❏ Aggressive ❏ Passive-Aggressive

7.   You have the right not to feel guilty
      ❏ Assertive ❏ Passive ❏ Aggressive ❏ Passive-Aggressive

8.   You have the right to say no.
      ❏ Assertive ❏ Passive ❏ Aggressive ❏ Passive-Aggressive

9.   The world is a dangerous place, it is best to keep quiet.
      ❏ Assertive ❏ Passive ❏ Aggressive ❏ Passive-Aggressive

10.   Just in case your anger and frustration is not justified, it is better to express it in such a way that others won't know who is responsible.
      ❏ Assertive ❏ Passive ❏ Aggressive ❏ Passive-Aggressive

11.   If you compromise, you won't get what you want.
      ❏ Assertive ❏ Passive ❏ Aggressive ❏ Passive-Aggressive

12.   If people are punished, they will figure out on their own what they did wrong.
      ❏ Assertive ❏ Passive ❏ Aggressive ❏ Passive-Aggressive

13.   It's really not that important.
      ❏ Assertive ❏ Passive ❏ Aggressive ❏ Passive-Aggressive

14.   You must win in order for others to accept you.
      ❏ Assertive ❏ Passive ❏ Aggressive ❏ Passive-Aggressive

15.   You have the right to have and express feelings, even those that others might not approve of.
      ❏ Assertive ❏ Passive ❏ Aggressive ❏ Passive-Aggressive

16.   Others can usually figure out what you want, think, or feel.
      ❏ Assertive ❏ Passive ❏ Aggressive ❏ Passive-Aggressive

17.   You have the right to change your mind.
      ❏ Assertive ❏ Passive ❏ Aggressive ❏ Passive-Aggressive

18.   If you can't get what you want, get even.
      ❏ Assertive ❏ Passive ❏ Aggressive ❏ Passive-Aggressive

19.   If you are honest with others, they will retaliate.
      ❏ Assertive ❏ Passive ❏ Aggressive ❏ Passive-Aggressive

20.   You have the right to ask fo help and for what you want.
      ❏ Assertive ❏ Passive ❏ Aggressive ❏ Passive-Aggressive

21.   Things will get better on their own
      ❏ Assertive ❏ Passive ❏ Aggressive ❏ Passive-Aggressive

22.   Asking for something is selfish and needlessly inconveniences others. It is better just to keep your wants to yours.
      ❏ Assertive ❏ Passive ❏ Aggressive ❏ Passive-Aggressive

23.   You have the right to be less than what others expect of you.
      ❏ Assertive ❏ Passive ❏ Aggressive ❏ Passive-Aggressive

24.   People who hold in their own wants, thoughts, and feelings are more likable.
      ❏ Assertive ❏ Passive ❏ Aggressive ❏ Passive-Aggressive

25.   You should feel terribly guilty if something you say happens to bother others
      ❏ Assertive ❏ Passive ❏ Aggressive ❏ Passive-Aggressive

26.   You are responsible when others feel hurt.
      ❏ Assertive ❏ Passive ❏ Aggressive ❏ Passive-Aggressive

27.   It is dangerous to express anger in such a way
      that you can be identified.
      ❏ Assertive ❏ Passive ❏ Aggressive ❏ Passive-Aggressive

28.   The best way to respect others is not to make
      waves and express yourself.
      ❏ Assertive ❏ Passive ❏ Aggressive ❏ Passive-Aggressive

29.   If you express your feelings, others will think
      you are too aggressive or misunderstand your
      intentions.
      ❏ Assertive ❏ Passive ❏ Aggressive ❏ Passive-Aggressive

30.   People who say things that end up hurting you
      do so deliberately, or are evil.
      ❏ Assertive ❏ Passive ❏ Aggressive ❏ Passive-Aggressive

31.   People won't take you seriously, or think you
      are a real man (or woman) unless you are
      tough.
      ❏ Assertive ❏ Passive ❏ Aggressive ❏ Passive-Aggressive

32.   People who don't come on strong aren't listened
      too.
      ❏ Assertive ❏ Passive ❏ Aggressive ❏ Passive-Aggressive

2. What's your assertive reply?

Here are some situations. For each indicate if the
described response is assertive, passive, aggressive, or
passive-aggressive. Then give your own assertive reply.

Situation 1: The Cancelled Trip

You and your roommate have planned to go on a trip to
the woods. Unexpectedly, your friend calls and cancels.
You say: "Gee. This is really unexpected. I need some
time to think about where this puts me. Let me call you
back"

Is this:

❏ Assertive ❏ Passive ❏ Aggressive ❏ Passive-Aggressive

If this is not assertive, what would be an assertive
alternative?

Situation 2: Pigpen Roommate

Your roommate leaves the kitchen in a mess whenever
she uses it. Dirty dishes are piled up in the sink. Open
food in rotting in the fridge. Food is left on the stove.
You say: "This pig pen is a mess! Just like you! How
can you live with yourself? You must be more considerate
of others."

Is this:

❏ Assertive ❏ Passive ❏ Aggressive ❏ Passive-Aggressive

If this is not assertive, what would be an assertive
alternative?

Situation 3: Tacos or Hotrods

Your girl/boyfriend wants to watch a rerun of a cooking show on making bean tacos. You really want to watch a special on hotrods.

You say: "Oh, honey. You can watch your taco show. I don't really want to watch my special show anyway. It really doesn't mean that much to me. The way you cook, you need as much help as you can get."

Is this:

❑ Assertive ❑ Passive ❑ Aggressive ❑ Passive-Aggressive

If this is not assertive, what would be an assertive alternative?

Situation 4: Oily Kid

Your 12-year old son just finished fixing his bike and hasn't picked up all the dirt and oil he left behind. You step in the mess and get your white shoes dirty.

You say: "You are the most inconsiderate kid I know. You just don't think about how your actions affect others."

Is this:

❑ Assertive ❑ Passive ❑ Aggressive ❑ Passive-Aggressive

If this is not assertive, what would be an assertive alternative?

Situation 5: Bully Girls

Your son gets punched out by a bunch of big girls several times each week just after school. You are concerned that his grade school teacher hasn't done anything about it. You have a meeting with the teacher.

You say: "My son got hit three times this week, and twice last week after school. This is not acceptable, especially since I have written the school principle about the problem. I must insist that something be done. When can we meet so we can come up with an answer?"

Is this:

❑ Assertive ❑ Passive ❑ Aggressive ❑ Passive-Aggressive

If this is not assertive, what would be an assertive alternative?

Situation 6: The Secretary Issue

You are the only guy in a church group of 12 women. The group has to discuss church finances. Before the meeting, they have to select a secretary. The women turn to you and say, "We gals have done this type of work all our lives. It's time a man is secretary. You're it!"

You say: "Hey, I understand your concerns about discrimination against women. But let's be fair. You're guilty of reverse discrimination. Wouldn't it be more reasonable to rotate the job, so everyone gets to do it once?"

Is this:

❑ Assertive ❑ Passive ❑ Aggressive ❑ Passive-Aggressive

If this is not assertive, what would be an assertive alternative?

Situation 7: Overtime Bummer

You have worked overtime every day this week, often missing dinner. Your boss asks you to work on Saturday, even though that is your official day off..

You say: "Ooo, that hurts. Sure, I'll come in. Sure.

Is this:

❑ Assertive ❑ Passive ❑ Aggressive ❑ Passive-Aggressive

If this is not assertive, what would be an assertive alternative?

Situation 8: Help! Here Comes Mom!

Your mother wants to visit you on Saturday, the same day you have planned a special trip to the park with your friends. She springs this on you at the last moment. She lives only a mile away from you.

You say: "Mom, I need to have my own time. I'm 23 and not your little kid anymore. You need to respect this."

Is this:

❑ Assertive ❑ Passive ❑ Aggressive ❑ Passive-Aggressive

If this is not assertive, what would be an assertive alternative?

Situation 9: The Drug Bust

Your buddy wants you to do cocaine with him. You tried it, but have made a firm decision not to do any more. Your buddy insists and accuses you of being not cool and not liking him anymore.

You say: "Listen, buddy, I hope we're still friends. But I've made a decision that's right for me. I want you to respect that."

Is this:

❑ Assertive ❑ Passive ❑ Aggressive ❑ Passive-Aggressive

If this is not assertive, what would be an assertive alternative?

Situation 10: Late Date

You have planned a date at a nice local pizza restaurant. Your date is 20 minutes late, and arrives with no excuse. You don't have access to a phone and feel pissed off.

You say: "Why are you always late? Do you have any idea how I feel?

Is this:

❑ Assertive ❑ Passive ❑ Aggressive ❑ Passive-Aggressive

If this is not assertive, what would be an assertive alternative?

Situation 11: Shovy Shopper

You are waiting in a long line at the drugstore to pay for your one bottle of orange soda. A middle aged lady in a nice suit shoves in front of you and pays for her things out of turn.

You say: "Excuse me, lady, I'm sorry I was taking up your space. Maybe I could carry your things out to your car for you."

Is this:

❏ Assertive ❏ Passive ❏ Aggressive ❏ Passive-Aggressive

If this is not assertive, what would be an assertive alternative?

Situation 12: The Wonderful Book

A friend who often borrows money without returning it asks for $40 to buy a hot new book on Stress Management he saw in the bookstore. You have the money in your pocket, but really don't want to give him any more until he pays back what he owes you.

You say: "Gosh, I wish I could help you. Please ask me later."

Is this:

❏ Assertive ❏ Passive ❏ Aggressive ❏ Passive-Aggressive

If this is not assertive, what would be an assertive alternative?

Situation 13: To Close for Comfort

Someone you like and have known for a year wants to thank you for your gift. This person touches you in a way that is a bit too intimate and makes you uncomfortable.

You say: "I'll have to charge you $50 for that."

Is this:

❏ Assertive ❏ Passive ❏ Aggressive ❏ Passive-Aggressive

If this is not assertive, what would be an assertive alternative?

Situation 14: Embarrassed at Work

Your work supervisor has criticized your performance in front of other workers. You feel really embarrassed and wish she wouldn't have done that.

You say: "I have a request. Sometimes it is helpful to get your feedback about my work, but could you possibly give it to me alone, and not in front of others. It makes me feel a little funny."

Is this:

❏ Assertive ❏ Passive ❏ Aggressive ❏ Passive-Aggressive

If this is not assertive, what would be an assertive alternative?

Situation 15: Beer Boy

You live in a dormitory and enjoy the party your floor has every month. However, you are always the one who has to go out and buy the beer. Sometimes you get reimbursed, sometimes only partly reimbursed. However, you are the best choice to get the beer given that your family's home is right next to the store.

You say: "You know, you guys still owe me some money. This is getting a little tiresome."

Is this:

❏ Assertive ❏ Passive ❏ Aggressive ❏ Passive-Aggressive

If this is not assertive, what would be an assertive alternative?

3. Your Situation

Think of a situation in which you were not as assertive as you might have been. Describe all the details.

Then present an assertive alternative, including what you would say.

List the costs and benefits of what actually happened and the assertive alternative.

Your situation. What happened?

Costs	Benefits

Assertive Option

Costs	Benefits

CHAPTER 27
SUPER-ASSERTIVENESS: MAKING DIFFICULT REQUESTS

Sometimes it is not enough to assertively state what is on your mind. Some situations call for a more powerful approach, **super- assertiveness**.

Super-assertiveness can be used when you are making a difficult request, that is, asking for something another person may not want to give. This can include asking another person to change or stop what they are doing, do something new, or give something they may hesitate giving: Life is filled with situations calling for difficult requests, for example:

- *You are waiting in a grocery store checkout line. Someone has clumsily stepped in front of you. You want to bring this to their attention.*
- *Time is ready for a raise or promotion. You have decided to ask for one.*
- *It is Sunday and your neighbors are making far too much noise You want to ask them to quiet down.*
- *Your daughter comes home late every Saturday. You want that to stop.*
- *Your 8-year old son is using foul language, and you want him to change.*
- *You and your friend are spending the weekend together. However, you have different plans.*
- *You want to return an item purchased at a store.*
- *You want more time to pay back money to a friend.*
- *Your neighbor has not returned the frying pan he borrowed.*

Consider super assertiveness when:

- There is a good chance your request may not be heard or taken seriously.
- You are dealing with someone who may misunderstand what you are saying or take your requests the wrong way (as an insult or joke, for example).
- Your request is very important and you want to maximize the likelihood that it will be honored.
- There is a possibility of a hostile reply.

- You want to establish an atmosphere of openness and honesty (for example, with a spouse or friend).

The Key to Super-Assertiveness
The DESC Script

The key to super-assertiveness is to go beyond assertively stating what is on your mind; instead, you carefully spell out all the facts relevant to the situation. For example, if you want a friend to return your bicycle, a simple assertion might go like this:

I want my bike back, please.

But imagine your friend has a habit of not returning what he borrows, doesn't seem to take your requests seriously, and sometimes blames you of picking on him when you do ask for your things back. Then you might try a super-assertion:

Last Monday you borrowed my bike and promised to return it the next day. One week has passed, and I feel really frustrated and a bit irritated. I want my bike today. Hey, I need my bike today to visit my mother. And frankly, I'm getting a little tired of lending you things and not knowing when I'll get them back. You're my friend, and I want to help you when you ask, but you make it hard by not returning things.

A Super-assertion lays all the facts on the table – what the problem is, how you feel about it, what you want, and what's going to happing. Bower and Bower (1991) offer a classic tool for doing this – the **DESC script**. There are four steps:

Describe. Clearly and objectively state the other person's behavior or words that are an issue to you or a problem.

Express. State your thoughts and feelings in reaction to the described behavior.

Specify. Make a specific, concrete request.

Consequences. Outline the positive consequences for oneself and the other person if the request is followed.

Examples

Helping a Friend Type Assignments

Describe. *For five days in a week you have asked me to type your homework for you. Each assignment takes about an hour. I notice that you have not attended your typing class for a month.*

Express. *I am beginning to feel frustrated at doing all this work. I feel like I am being used and that you aren't doing your share.*

Specify. *I want you to start going back to typing class and start typing your assignments tomorrow.*

Consequences. *If you can do at least some of your typing yourself, I'll be happy to help you do more*

Eating My Food

Describe. *Wednesday I did my grocery shopping and put my week's food in the bottom shelf of our shared refrigerator. I saw you eating my food yesterday and today, so it's almost gone.*

Express. *This gets me angry. We share the same refrigerator so we have to respect each other's food space.*

Specify. *Please eat your food, and if you want to eat some of mine, ask.*

Consequences. *That way I'll know if I have enough to eat this week. I won't have to worry about where my food is going. And I won't get angry.*

DESC Script Do's and Don'ts

Describe

Describe the other person's behavior, not your own feelings. Don't get overemotional; just stick to the facts. Use concrete terms, stating who, when, what, and where. Don't guess at the other person's feelings or reasons.

✓ **Correct:** *Yesterday at noon you promised to meet me for breakfast. You did not arrive.*
   Incorrect: *I am upset because you did not show up for breakfast today as you promised.*
✓ **Correct:** *Last week you complained to the supervisor that I have been answering your phone calls.*

   Incorrect: *Please address your complaints to me in the future rather than to my supervisor.*
✓ **Correct:** *This lamp I purchased yesterday doesn't light up when I turn it on.*
   Incorrect: *I want a new lamp. This one is junk!*

Express

Calmly state your own feelings, relating them to the specific behavior, not the whole person.

✓ **Correct::** *I am frustrated and a little confused by your not showing up for breakfast.*
   Incorrect:: *You know, I would appreciate it if you could be a little more considerate of your friends.*
✓ **Correct:** *Frankly, I an irritated and angry .*
   Incorrect: *Frankly, please keep your feelings to yourself.*
✓ **Correct:** *I was disappointed when I found this out.*
   Incorrect: *I feel you should check more carefully the merchandise you sell.*

Specify

Ask for realistic concrete, behavioral change, indicating again who, what, when, and where. Acknowledge the other person's wants.

✓ **Correct:** *Next time you can't make a breakfast date, at least call me on your cell phone.*
   Incorrect: *I want you to be more considerate of the concerns and time of your friends.*
✓ **Correct::** *I understand we may have disagreements. I think it is fair to ask that if you have concerns about things I am doing, you bring them up to me.*
   Incorrect: *You are not contributing to a good work environment. I feel uncomfortable working with you.*
✓ **Correct:** *I simply want a new lamp for the defective one.*
   Incorrect: *Correct this immediately*

Consequences

Be honest, realistic, concrete, and explicit. Don't bribe, threaten, or promise too much.

✓ **Correct::** *We'll call each other if we can't show up. At least I'll know what's going on and won't worry.*
   Incorrect: *Don't worry. I still like you!*
✓ **Correct:** *I enjoy working with you, and will certainly feel I can trust you to be honest with me.*
   Incorrect: *You know, there's lot's of stuff I could complain to the boss about you.*

✓ **Correct:** *If we can work this out, I will certainly enjoy continue shopping here.*
Incorrect: *You have to replace the defective lamp I bought here.*

The Positive DESC Script

One way of making a good DESC script more effective is to precede it with a compliment. However make sure your compliment is honest, specific, and related to the request you wish to make. For example, imagine you are returning an item to a store for a refund. You are not completely sure you will get a refund. A positive DESC script might go like this:

I enjoy shopping at your store. Last week I was really pleased with how courteous and prompt your service was.

However, I do have a request. The lamp I purchased is broken. It simply doesn't work. I was a bit frustrated because of the long trip I made just to come to this store. I would like a refund, and would feel much relieved if I could receive it today so I could continue shopping.

Note how the beginning compliment is specific (it identifies why the person was pleased). And it is relevant, related to the store and its service. The following Positive DESC Script has a problem. It isn't specific or particularly relevant. Can you see why?

John, we've been friends for over a year. You are a really nice person.

Last week you borrowed my CD player and promised to return it the next day. I still don't have it and am getting worried. I need my CD player for my party tonight. I would like to have it today. I really want my party to be hot!

CHAPTER 26 EXERCISES

1. What's wrong with these scripts?

The most frequent mistake in creating DESC scripts is getting lines mixed up. People frequently put Describe line information in a Specify line, express emotions in a Describe line, and so on. See if you can identify how these lines are mixed up. Then for each create a correct DESC script.

Poor Service

Waitress, I'm sorry, but I am getting really frustrated about your service. I am seriously considering never coming here again for a meal. I have waiting over 20 minutes for service.

Describe

Express

Specify

Consequences

Party Drinker

I am going to have to ask you to leave if you don't stop drinking. You have had 12 beers in the last hour and our party has just started. I think you've had your limit, so please, no more beer. I've reached my limit.

Describe

Express

Specify

Consequences

2. Missing information

Another mistake people make with DESC scripts is leaving out important information, or not presenting information in a way that is concrete and specific (What, Where, When, Who). Here are some scripts with missing information. Indicate what is missing and give an example of the type of information that is needed.

The Book Salesman Who Will Not Stop

Listen, I don't want your stupid book. Leave me alone. What part of "no" do you not understand?

The Cheating Boyfriend

I think you are no longer interested in me. Maybe we should call it quits. I just get the feeling your interests are elsewhere.

3. Your DESC script

Think of a difficult request you have had to make of another person. Present this request in terms of a DESC script.

Your Situation:

Describe

Express

Specify

Consequences

4. Your Positive DESC Script

Now try writing a Positive DESC Script. Make sure your beginning compliment is honest, specific, and relevant.

Your Situation:

COMPLIMENT:

Describe:

Express:

Specify:

Consequences

5. Costs and Benefits

What are the costs and benefits of using a DESC script?

Costs	Benefits

What are the costs and benefits of using a Positive DESC script?

Costs	Benefits

6. Fix this DESC Script

What's wrong with this script? Fix it, please.

OSCAR WORKS AT A TACO STAND WITH HIS BROTHER, EDEL. FOR THE LAST FIVE WEEKS HIS BROTHER HAS PROMISED TO PAY HIM. HOWEVER, OSCAR HAS YET TO BE PAID. HE DECIDES T CONFRONT HIS BROTHER WITH A DESC SCRIPT. HERE IT IS. EVALUATE AND REWRITE EACH STEP.

D: "Edel, I'm pissed off. You've been taking me for granted for too long. I feel like I'm your servant. We agreed that this would be a business arrangement, an actual job. Instead, I feel like I'm doing you a favor, helping you out with cooking. It's always this way. I have to do all your chores, at work and at home too."

E: "What I want is really simple. I just want you to treat me with a little respect. Is that too much to ask? Just don't treat me like an unpaid servant. Everyone needs some recognition."

S: I can't continue under these conditions. You're going to make me quit. Then what will you do? I'd like to see how you get along in life without your little Oscar!

C: I don't know why I'm even telling you this. You never listen. But get this: if you keep treating me like your pet puppy, some day this doggie is going to bite back!!

YOUR COMMENTS AND CORRECTIONS

CHAPTER 28
SHYNESS AND STARTING RELATIONSHIPS

This chapter considers a special type of stress, that which arises from not making and pursuing relationships -- or shyness. There are many excellent books on shyness (Antony & Swinson, 2000;Bower & Bower, 1991; Curran, Wallander, & Farrell, 1985; Hope, Heimberg, Juster, & Turk, 2000;Jakubowski & Lange, 1978; and West, Goethe, & Kallman, 1980). The most popular strategy is to cultivate brainstorming new ways of meeting people, following up an introduction, ending a conversations, and dealing with rejection. The ideas generated can then be combined with relaxation, rethinking resistance to taking action, and desensitization, all topics covered elsewhere in the this book.

Brainstorming Ways of Meeting People

We begin with a setting where there are opportunities for meeting others, for example, at work, at school, in a lunchroom, a pub, a party, or church or temple. If you need help in thinking of meeting places, try brainstorming (Chapter 15).

Distorted thinking. Often it is hard to take the first step and introduce yourself. Typically, a distorted belief or excess tension gets in the way. You may harbor such unrealistic thoughts as assuming others will reject you, thinking you will appear foolish, assuming it is a very terrible thing if you indeed appear foolish, fearing that the person will not be your ideal match and you will have difficulty getting out of the conversation, and so on. Identify and do a reality check on whatever thoughts may interfere (Chapters 19-21).

Relaxation. Spot relaxation is an ideal way of preparing for taking the first step and meeting someone. First you need to learn your preferred forms of relaxation, and then select a mini-relaxation to use before your meeting. You might, for example, take a few slow deep breaths, stretch a few times, or entertain a brief positive fantasy (Chapter 10-11).

Desensitization. If meeting others causes enough tension and anxiety that you either avoid the task or bungle your attempts, then a little preliminary practice through desensitization (Chapter 23) might be useful. I recommend a variation called *in vivo* ("live") desensitization. The idea is to practice meeting others in very safe and nonthreatening settings (real, live settings, rather than those that are imagined), and practice relaxation while doing this. First, identify some practice meeting rehearsal tasks, and rank them from easy to difficult. For example, one brief hierarchy might include:

1. Go to a party with a friend and meet someone he/she introduces you to.
2. Introduce yourself to three people who pose no threat to you. Pick people you probably will never meet again. These should be people who's opinion of you doesn't matter at all. Whether they think you are silly, pushy, uninteresting, or stupid, should mean little to you, because (a) you aren't going to reveal anything seriously personal and (b) you will never see them again. Then plan your opening lines and some lines of conversation very carefully.
3. Play a game with a friend at school in which both of you seee how many people you can meet in an hour. The winner buys dinner.
4. Practice with a friend. Explain that you want to role play meeting and using opening lines, with him/her playing the part of the person being met.

Opening Lines:: What to Say First

Brainstorm and practice possible opening lines. An opening line doesn't have to be particularly profound, insightful, or clever. Indeed, openers that appear exceptionally polished can be threatening to others. Simple lines are best. One might want to first think of a set of opening lines. Here are researchers have found useful (Kleinke, Meeker, & Staneski, 1986):

"Hi."
"Can you give me directions to _____?"
"Can you help me with _____?"
"Did you see (name a movie or TV show)?"
"Have you read (name an article or book)?"
"I feel a bit embarrassed about this -- I'd like to meet you."
"That's a very pretty (sweater, shirt, etc.) you have on."
"You have really nice (hair, eyes, etc.)"
"Since we're both sitting alone, would you care to join me?"
"Is it OK if I sit with you?"

Less effective opening lines include:

"I'm easy. Are you?"
"I've got an offer you can't refuse."
"What's your sign?"
"Didn't we meet in a previous life?"
"Your place or mine?"
"Is that really your hair?"
"You remind me of a woman (man) I used to date."
"Isn't it cold? Let's make some body heat."
"What's that hanging from your nose?"

Your opening line should feel safe for yourself and the other person. Think of something that the other person can answer easily, or decline easily. Often experts recommend avoiding opening lines that:

* Include cute statements
* Involve asking inappropriately intimate or probing questions
* Fill the air with empty talk
* Put oneself down
* Involve perfunctory ice-breakers and waiting for the other person to jump in and save the conversation.

Asking an open-ended question can be a good opening line. An open-ended question is one that cannot be answered with a simple "yes" or "no." They make it very easy for the other person to continue the conversation. In contrast, simple "Yes / No" questions can be answered with a single "yes" or "no," often resulting in awkward silence. Here are some examples of open-ended questions:

"That's looks like an interesting magazine. What is that
     cover about?"
"What do you think about this place? I have mixed feelings."

Don't forget to think up what to say after your opening line.

Following up and Maintaining a Conversation.

Once you've started a conversation, it can be hard to continue. Some people worry about being too pushy or saying the wrong thing. Here are some hints others have suggested: (Conger & Farrell, 1981; Greenwald, 1977; Kukpke, Calhoun, & Hobbs, 1979):

* Can you tell if the other person really wants to continue the conversation? Are they giving you "free information" about themselves, such as what they think or feel. Are they smiling and facing you, or turning away, looking at their watch, yawning?
* Listen to what they are saying. Paraphrase the gist of what they are saying. This shows you are interested.

Antony and Swinson (2000) and McKay, Davis, and Fanning (1995) suggest some "don'ts" to avoid:

* Don't compare yourself to others. ("I make more money than my brother").
* Don't ignore key points of what the other person is saying.
* Don't abruptly change topics. This might be perceived as a rude, self-centered interruption.
* Don't overrehearse
* Don't "butter up" the other person. You might think that you can make other people like you more if you constantly agree with them or praise them. This might work with some people. It turns many people off.
* Avoid body language that suggests you don't like the other person or aren't interested. This may include leaning back in your chair, standing far away, avoiding eye contact, frowning, or crossing your arms.

Dealing with Rejection

Sometimes shy people avoid meeting others because of fear of rejection. If this is a concern, I recommend reading Chapters 19-21.

CHAPTER 27 EXERCISES

1. Observe Others.

Spend the week listening to others, both in real-life or in the movies or television. Pay particular attention to people who seem to be meeting someone for the first time. Take note of what they are saying and doing.

What are their opening lines? How would evaluate their opening lines using the concepts of this chapter? What good ideas did you note? Why were they good? What strategies did you notice that weren't so good? Why?

Good Ideas

Why?

Not so Good Ideas

W/hy?

Look at their body language and nonverbal cues. Describe the appropriateness and impact of what you note.

2.   When have you been shy?

Think of several situations in which you could have tried to meet others, but did not. What were you thinking? Did any of your thoughts get in the way?

3. Shyness Practice

Think of some safe situations where you can practice meeting others and using opening lines. Rank these from easy to more challenging.:

Difficult and challenging practice situations

Moderate-level difficulty situations

Easy practice situations

4. Opening Lines.

Brainstorm some possible opening lines as well as follow-up lines. Ask your friends and people you know what works best for them. For each, indicate wether it is an "open ended" or "yes-no" opening line. Rank them according to which you think are best for you.

Dealing with Rejection

What distorted, negative thoughts are you most likely to think when someone you are meeting for the first time rejects you? See Chapters 19 and 209. Describe your thought, and then assess how realistic it is, including a more realistic counter thought.

CHAPTER 29
TURNING YOUR ANGER INTO POWERFUL COPING

Do you ever get angry and later regret it? Do some of your conversations quickly turn into heated arguments? Do you sometimes "fly of the handle," only to later regret it? Do you sometimes think of yourself as a "touchy" or "irritable" person? These are just some of the signs of an anger-prone person. In this chapter we examine some powerful skills for transforming the wasted energy of anger and aggression into productive coping.

Use your Anger Early Warning Alarm

To convert wasted anger energy into productive coping, you need to catch anger in the bud, before it builds. It is easier to redirect the flow of a river close to its source rather than at the end point where it flows into a waterfall. It is easier to put out a fire in the wastebasket than to wait until the whole house is up in flames.

To catch anger in the bud, you need to discover your anger early warning alarms, the early warning signs that anger might build. It makes no sense having a fire alarm when you don't know what it sounds like. You may think that a whining siren is from some car across the street when in fact the wastebasket is burning. Here are some common anger alarm signs (Smith, 2002):

1. Someone else has, or is about to violate your expectations of what is right and expected
2. Someone else has, or is about to insult, hurt, or provoke another person significant to you
3. Someone else has, or is about to insult, hurt, or provoke you
4. You have met a serious frustration to your goals
5. You have encountered an appropriate target for expressing irrational/habitual or religion-based feelings of prejudice, bigotry, homophobia, or dislike

Any of these thoughts may be a good early anger alarms.

When you are closer to erupting with anger, your emotions and body may provide you with urgent warning signs. Emotional cues include, of course, feelings of anger, hostility, irritation, frustration, rage, and so on. Physiological cues of anger arousal include those related to muscle tension (making a fist, raising one's shoulders, puffing up one's chest, tightening ones muscles, standing tall, frowning, furrowing one's brow, clenching and grinding one's teeth, squinting, etc.) Other cues are related to breathing (holding one's breath) and arousal (rapid heart beat, stomach difficulties, feeling warm).

Early Coping Strategies
(Catching Anger in the Bud)

Once your anger alarm has suggested a problem about to arise, early coping strategies can quickly turn the potential of wasted anger into productive energy.

Relaxation. Relaxation can be an effective early anger-reducer. Simply counting to 10 is the easiest for many people. I suggest passive breathing exercises or progressive muscle relaxation. A simple breathing exercise might include: (Smith, 2002)

Let yourself breathe easily and naturally. When you are ready, take in a full deep breath, filling your lungs and abdomen with good, refreshing air. Pause. And when you are ready, relax. And slowly let the air flow out, very smoothly and gently. And now, just continue breathing normally for a while.

Reality Checking. Much anger is the result of unrealistic expectations, distorted perceptions, or failure to consider all the possible causes of a problem. Simply pausing, and taking time to consider all aspects of a provocative situation, can be enough to reduce the potential for anger.

Novoco's Anger Management Program

The above strategies are useful at those times you unexpectedly encounter a provoking situation. Novaco (1975) has proposed an anger management program that can be useful when you can anticipate ahead a possible provocative situation that is likely to arouse excessive anger. He suggests breaking a potential anger situation into four stages:

Preparing for provocation (pre-stress). Prepare ahead for possible provocation. Preparations should include **active coping plans**, specific courses of action you can take ("I can plan what to do ahead," "I can call my supervisor," "I can repeat my main point", possible **reality checks** that identify and defuse distorted thoughts ("I need to remember that a criticism of my behavior isn't necessarily a personal attack," "I might blow this out of perspective, so I should maintain perspective of what is important and what is not", and **relaxation and defensive strategies** to reduce or avoid tension ("I can do my breathing exercises," "I can just excuse myself and leave the situation")

Impact and confrontation (onset-stress). Plan what you will do when your provocative incident is just beginning The confrontation has occurred. Once again, you may consider active coping strategies, realistic and practical appraisal, and relaxation and defensive strategies.

Coping with arousal (mid-stress). When the confrontation is well underway, you unexpected anger. Again, plan ahead with active coping, reality-checking, and relaxation/defensive strategies.

Reflecting on the provocation (post-stress). Anticipate what happens after the confrontation. Think about what you will think and do if the conflict is resolved, or unresolved?

CHAPTER 28 EXERCISES

1. Anger Early Warning Signs.

What are your anger early warning alarms? If you can't think of any, describe a recent provocation in which you responded with too much anger. Describe the details, the When, Where, What, and Who. What did you want? Then, think about the time just before this provocation. Can you detect any ways you could have figured out that the situation was about to happen, or turn angry?

2. A Recent Provocation.

Think of a recent angry provocation, one in which you exploded with excessive anger. What distorted or unrealistic thoughts contribute to your anger? See Chapter 20.

CHAPTER 30
DEALING WITH AGGRESSION

Making difficult requests can be especially challenging when the possibility of aggression is involved. In these situations you are either responding to a threat of attack, or are making a request that may trigger verbal or physical violence.

The first goal of dealing with aggressive and manipulative behavior is to conduct a reality check and determine if the aggression or manipulation is real or imagined. What more information do you need in order to decide? If the threat is real, a number of experts (Goldstein & Keller, 1987; Jakubowski & Lange, 1987) suggest strategies for limiting the other person's aggressive behavior and dealing with the threat in general. These strategies involve:

• Introducing calm
• Getting to the source of the problem.

Introducing Calm (Smith, 2001)

Goldstein and Keller (1987) offer some very useful advice for relaxing a potentially hostile or aggressive person. I have somewhat revised their suggestions on the following pages:

Change to a neutral and more relaxed setting. Imagine a coworker has accused you of being rude and argumentative . Both of you are standing next to his office desk. People are waiting outside for their appointments with both of you. The pressure is building. Clearly this is not the time or place to sort things out. Suggest a neutral and quiet setting, perhaps over coffee at the local coffee house after work.

Model calmness. If you make a simple effort to be relaxed, this can help introduce an atmosphere of calm. Note your voice and posture. With a relaxed posture your shoulders are loose and slightly sloped. Your arms, hands, and legs are slightly open and not clenched. You aren't fidgeting or holding on to something tightly.

Be careful not to do a visible relaxation exercise during a threatening encounter (by deliberately taking slow deep breaths, tensing up and releasing

tension, or closing your eyes to meditate). These efforts work best before a potential encounter when one is alone. When done during an encounter, they can be misinterpreted as behavior that is hostile or defensive.

During an encounter, take a relaxed posture. Do not cross your arms, make a fist, or clench your teeth. Let yourself breathe in a relaxed way. If you notice your shoulders or arms getting tense, just let go.

Encourage rational and problem-solving talk. Set the stage for calm discussion by asking the other person what both of you might do to constructively deal with the problem. Note that if you ask the person to explain their anger, that may actually increase their anger ("Isn't it obvious, stupid . . . "). You might ask, "If you speak more slowly and quietly, I can understand you better."

Listen empathically. Honestly attempt to paraphrase what the other person is saying. Make it clear you are interested and listening. At least restate or rephrase their comments. If possible, focus on underlying feelings. But do not dwell on feelings, because this might aggravate anger. Move quickly to attempting to address the problem ("Now that I understand where you are coming from, let's get to business. What are our options?").

Reward calm behavior. Gently praise or reinforce the other person when they show less anger or aggression, and an increased willingness to engage in mature problem-solving. Try not to be patronizing. You might say, "Thanks for being open; that helps me know where you are coming from so we can work this thing out." "I appreciate your patience. I know this is difficult, but I want to solve this as quickly as you do."

Getting to the Source of the Problem

Ask for a clarification. Note if the angry person seems to be so overwhelmed with emotion that he or she ignores the specific problem. Simply acknowledge the emotion ("I can tell you are really irritated") and quickly focus on what you understand the concrete problem to be.

Focus on the concrete issue. Try to consistently approach your problem using the skills of problem-solving. That is, focus on what do you realistically want? What can you realistically seek for now? When do you want it? Where?

The other person may engage in emotional outburst, blaming, self-pity, and so on. Such efforts obscure the issue or divert attention from the real problem. Basically, acknowledge and respect what the other person is saying, and then suggest that it would be better for both of you to get right to the real problem. Then suggest your perception of the concrete issues that need to be addressed.

Tell the other person the message you hear. Honestly let the other person know the message that you are getting.

Person A: " *So far, what I have heard is that I am 'ruthless, insensitive, and arrogant.'" I'm confused. That doesn't tell me exactly what I need to do to help fix the problem."*

Person B: "It's your insensitivity to the rules we have at work."

Person A: "The rules? That helps somewhat, but which rules are you talking about?

Person B: "We all have to be here at 8:30 AM. Yesterday you were here at 9 AM. In fact every day last week you came in after 9 AM. That upsets me."

When Problem-Solving Doesn't Work

Sometimes, problem-solving is going nowhere and is clearly escalating to dangerous proportions. At some point one may have to take emergency action to defuse the situation. The ideas of this chapter can be applied to such emergencies. Specifically:

- Ask questions to prompt awareness of their aggressive behavior.
- Behave in a calm, problem-solving manner, in direct contrast to   the aggressive behavior being displayed.
- Provide direct and specific negative feedback.
- Treat a putdown as a neutral comment (ignore the emotional component, and focus on what might be true).
- Sort out fact from judgement and interpretation. Focus on the facts
- Announce the intent to escalate your assertions, and wish for a contract to end the aggression.

Some differences simply cannot be reconciled

and both parties may have to settle with accepting no resolution. Here, a reasonable goal can be to assertively express oneself, rethink one's goals, and go on living. One might choose to terminate an unsuccessful negotiation with a clear and concise summary of what has transpired, focusing on both one's own wants, thoughts, feelings, and behavior as well as those of the other person. Again, a DESC script (Chapter 26) can be a useful tool, with the Describe line focusing on the failed negotiation process:

Describe (Summarizes both positions):"We have negotiated this problem for three days. Both of us have made a reasonable attempt to offer solutions and compromises. But we still haven't reached a solution."

Express (What you feel): "I feel very frustrated when I can't negotiate a solution. But I also feel resigned that perhaps that is how it will have to be."

Specify (Make specific request): "Let me suggest that we stop our negotiations and accept that we both have legitimate, but irreconcilable, differences."

Consequences: "I would like to leave at least feeling that we made our best effort to resolve our differences, and that we still respect each other."

CHAPTER 29 EXERCISES

1. What's going on in this angry encounter?

On the following page is a tense exchange between Gil and Lois, a couple that has been married for about a year. Identify what techniques for reducing the potential for aggression are illustrated. Which are working? Which could use some improvement

THE FAMILY VISIT	YOUR ANALYSIS
Gil has just announced to Lois that is mother and family are coming to stay with them for a week. Lois is extremely upset and is close to moving out, or worse. **Lois**: How could you do such a thing? Don't you care for me at all? Everyday something like this happens. You constantly do things without asking or telling me. You just don't love me any more! How can I put up with this anymore? **Gil:** (Takes a deep breath, and sits down. Invites Lois to sit) You're really getting upset, and I understand that. I'm not sure what the issue is for you really. **Lois**: You don't? It's simple. You're always too inconsiderate and I can't take it any more. Stupid! **Gil.** Please help me out. Inconsiderate? I need some specifics. **Lois.** You know. You just don't talk to me anymore, like you don't care. **Gil.** This isn't helping. I can see you're upset. That's making me upset, and I don't think we can sort this out when we're both so stirred up. **Lois:** You asked your parents to stay with us for a week. You didn't ask me. What am I going to do? How am I supposed to feel? Do you want me to just obey all of your commands? **Gil:** One thing at a time, otherwise I get confused. Its hard for me to deal with name-calling, although I understand how you feel. I hear you saying you're angry I asked my parents to stay without talking to you first. Am I getting the point?	

Lois: Duhh. Yes, that's exactly it. And you're a selfish pig to boot.

Gil: I apologize for not asking you, and I know you're frustrated. I promise I will ask you in the future. But I'm not sure that is all that's going on here.

Lois: Isn't it obvious? Where are they going to stay? Who is going to feed them? Where are we going to put our four children? And we're going on vacation two weeks from now. How can we plan with your parents always around

Gil: I guess I hadn't thought that through. By the way, it helps when you explain to me exactly what's going on. I can think things through more clearly. But I'm not sure where to begin. You and I have a problem, and I'm really sorry I caused it. But what's done is done? Where do you suggest we begin?

Lois: Well, for starters, is it a done deal that they're coming? Have they bought their plane tickets? Could their trip be delayed until after our vacation? Is there any chance they could stay in the motel on the corner?

Gil: Hmm, those concrete ideas get me thinking. There's got to be an answer to this. Maybe I could call them up today and tell them the situation, and see what kind of compromise we all can live with.

Lois: Yes, I think we should call them up as soon as possible. But I also think we should think through ahead of time what we want, what we can live with, and what just won't work with them. If we call them and treat this as just one of those unexpected problems that happen, we can figure it out at mature adults.

Gil: Good idea. Let's start after breakfast. You know, you're so sexy when you're angry!

Lois: You pig!

2. Examples of Tense Encounters in Entertainment

Find a story, tv show, or movie that illustrates an angry encounter between at least two people. Show how it illustrates the concepts in this chapter.

3. Observations of Angry Encounters

This week keep your eye out for an angry or aggressive encounter. Carefully note which of the ideas of this chapter are illustrated.

4.. Your Angry Encounter

Think of a recent angry encounter that either went well or didn't go so well. Describe the encounter. Explain which ideas in this chapter are illustrated.

PART VI
STRESS AND LIFE

CHAPTER 31
NUTRITION AND EXERCISE

About half of the many dozens of books on stress include suggestions on how to reduce or prevent stress by making general changes in one's lifestyle and environment. We find chapters on leisure, nutrition, exercise, study habits, the environment, community living, volunteering, and so on. At this point it is important to make some important distinctions.

First, stress management involves learning to deal with stressors, generally through problem-solving, rethinking, and relaxation, and specifically through applying various social skills such as assertiveness, as well as shyness and anger management.

Second, although all stressors may be viewed as challenges, not all challenges are stressors. Having a flat tire, getting married, planning a vacation, looking for a new apartment, cleaning up after a sick dog, may well be challenges calling for solutions. They are stressors only if they (1) are very much unwanted, uncontrollable, chronic, and call for serious life change and (2) evoke stress arousal /distress.

Third, anything you do to enhance happiness and health may enable you to be more resistant to stress and effectively use the coping resources you have. This point is often a source of confusion in stress management textbooks. If you are sick with the flu, it is likely you are not particularly happy. Ordinary life events are more likely to be seen as stressors and evoke stress arousal. For example, if, while sick in bed, your boss sends you an e-mail saying that your budget report is due the next day regardless of your condition – that assignment is a stressor. If you received the same assignment when feeling fit and energized, it would be a simple challenge. Although catching the flu was not a stressor, it set the stage for making other things stressful. And, most important, taking sensible steps to avoid the flu, for example, washing hands and avoiding sneezing children, obviously are not forms of stress management; they may prevent sickness that sets you up for stress. Taking steps to stay healthy and

happy may make you more resistant to stress; however, such steps should not be seen as stress management techniques. (one exception is when a wellness activity is used as a temporary diversion from a stressor.

This said, let us consider three major variables which, although not necessarily forms of stress management, can set the stage for effective stress management.

Nutrition

The food we eat consists of carbohydrates, fats, protein, and water. Eating proper quantities of the right foods helps contribute to physical health and psychological well-being, and enables you to prevent and stress more effectively. If you are starving or sick with an illness associated with obesity, you increase your risk for stress. The same is true if you do not maintain a diet best for you. Although some stress guides provide detailed advice on the "ideal diet," I feel such advice is out of place in a book on stress management. There is not one right diet for everyone. The right diet depends on your condition, whether you are a growing child, a diabetic, a marathon runner, a sumo wrestler, recovering from heart surgery, living with AIDS, trying to gain weight, trying to lose weight, and so on. However, there are some specific points worth noting:

- During periods of prolonged and severe stress (unemployment, war), your body may begin to consume protein in your muscles when you have used up stored carbohydrates and fats. Here it is important to eat well, ideally with smaller and more frequent meals, and drink plenty of fluids.
- It is possible that eating high levels of fat, sugar, and salt (Macht, 1996) increases stress reactivity.
- For some, consuming simple sugars (as in candy, many breakfast foods, cookies) results in hypoglycemia (low blood sugar level), a condition associated with fatigue, irritability, anxiety, and other conditions similar to stress.

- Serotonin is a neurotransmitter substance that influences how our brains and nervous system operate. Depressed people appear to have low levels of serotonin. Markus, Panhuysen, Tuiten, Koppenschaar, Fekkes, and Peters (1998) suggest that high levels of experienced stress may be associated with serotonin deficiencies, and that eating complex carbohydrates (fruits, vegetables, whole-grain products) may help moderate this problem.

- **Pseudostressors** (or sympathomimetics) are foods that produce a response that mimics sympathetic nervous system arousal. The most common pseudostressor is caffeine. Indeed, a five-ounce cup of coffee contains 150 mg of caffeine, very similar to the official clinical dose in drugs of 200mg. A lethal dose of caffeine can range from 2,000 or 10,000 mg. Other pseudostressors include:

> *Chocolate , Cocoa, Cola*
> *Energy drinks and bars*
> *Teas (black, green, and some herbal)*

Exercise

The fight or flight stress response gives us quick energy for vigorous emergency action. This automatic response served us well when we lived in caves and the jungle. Early humans, although frequently threatened, could frequently burn off their stress energy through fighting or fleeing. Today, civilized men and women do not have such daily opportunities to release stress energy. This bottled up stress energy makes us more vulnerable to stressors, and can contribute to stress-related illness. Regular and appropriate exercise can help correct this problem.

Benefits of Exercise

Physical effects. Vigorous physical activity helps burn off and release potentially harmful parts of the stress response. Muscle tension is released; after exercise, one may well experience deactivation of stress arousal through the physiological relaxation response. Stress-related hormones (adrenalin and cortisol) are spent, so less remains to create stress. Fats, including cholesterol, are broken down as fuel for action. Heart and lungs are exercised, increasing endurance and capacity.

Psychological effects. Vigorous exercise may release mood-elevating neurotransmitters, including endorphins, serotonin, and dopamine. These are the same brain chemicals that are responsible for the intense feelings of euphoria associated with various illegal mood-enhancing drugs. However, through exercise you trigger these neurotransmitters by yourself, without harmful side-effects. (Note that relaxation exercises discussed earlier may have similar effects.)

In addition, exercise may increase positive self-image (through loss of weight and improved physical condition) and ability to concentrate as well as reduce anxiety and depression.

Which Exercise?

It is beyond the scope of this text to prescribe a specific exercise program. I recommend first consulting with your physician, and then an exercise trainer. Generally, aerobic exercise (fast movement exercise such as running, walking, basketball, soccer, and so on) is preferred over anaerobic exercise (low-movement exercise such as weightlifting). Also, highly competitive sports can be counterproductive and create stress; noncompetitive vigorous activity is often better.

Different types of activity require different levels of exertion. The effectiveness of an exercise depends on how long you do it, how intense the activity is, and how frequently you practice. Most experts suggest beginning easy, and gradually building up to about three times a week. See the following table for the Surgeon General's guidelines on exercise.

Moderate Activity Guidelines (Exercises near the top of this list require more time because they are less vigorous)

Washing and waxing a car for 45-60 minutes
Washing windows or floors for 45-60 minutes
Playing volleyball for 45 minutes
Playing touch football for 30-45 minutes
Gardening for 30-45 minutes
Wheeling self in wheelchair for 30-40 minutes
Walking 1¾ miles in 35 minutes (20 min / mile)
Basketball (shooting baskets) for 30 minutes
Bicycling 5 miles in 30 minutes
Dancing fast (social) for 30 minutes
Pushing a stroller 1½ miles in 30 minutes
Raking leaves for 30 minutes
Walking 2 miles in 30 minutes (15 min/mile)
Doing water aerobics for 30 minutes
Swimming laps for 20 minutes
Playing wheelchair basketball for 20 minutes
Playing basketball for 15-20 minutes
Bicycling 4 miles in 15 minutes
Jumping rope for 15 minutes
Running 1 ½ miles in 15 minutes (10 min / mile)
Shoveling snow for 15 minutes
Stair walking for 15 minutes

Surgeon General of the United States (1999)

Precautions

Do not begin an exercise program without first consulting with your physician. A sudden increase in activity level can be fatal. The American College of Sports Medicine (ACSM; 1994) advises that physician's approval is especially important if:

- Your doctor has ever noted that you have a heart condition and physical activities should be medically supervised
- You have chest pains during or after exercising
- You have experienced a chest pain at least once in the previous month
- You have lost consciousness or fallen over because of dizziness at least once
- You have a medical condition affecting bones or joints that could be aggravated by physical activity
- You have ever been under treatment for hypertension or a heart condition
- You have, or have been told you have by a medical professional, any physical reason that might prohibit you from engaging in medically unsupervised exercise

In general, Everly and Lating (2002) recommend the following considerations:

- Physical exercise is in itself a serious stressor, one that can potentially evoke higher levels of physical stress than any other stressor. Starting exercise abruptly, without warmup or appropriate medical precautions, can trigger cardiac failure.
- The musculoskeletal system, including bones, muscles, joints, and tendons, are vulnerable to the strain of physical exertion. It is important to exercise with proper equipment using proper technique.
- Get advice on what type of exercise is best for you.
- Exercise works only when it is practiced consistently. It helps to do an exercise that is fun, perhaps involving other people.
- Some benefits may take several weeks or longer to emerge.

CHAPTER 32
THE ENVIRONMENT AND STRESS

The first stress researchers focused primarily on the environment, both internal and external. Although their notions that stress is a simple stressor-symptom equation are now outdated, some of their ideas concerning the environment are highly relevant today.

A Bit of History

Our notions of the physiology of stress evolved from the work of Claude Bernard, Walter Cannon and Hans Selye. Bernard was a French physiologist who in the late 1800's spoke of how the body attempts to maintain physiological balance, one's internal environment or **milieu interieur**, in face of changes in the outside environment. When the weather turns cold, the body's thermostat warms up. When the environment becomes hot and dry, the body conserves water. When the body does not automatically maintain internal balance in the face of changing environmental conditions, it can begin to suffer illness.

Cannon, a Harvard Physiologist, refined Bernard's ideas about 50 years later (Bernard, 1932). He introduced the notion of **homeostasis**. or normal state of internal functioning (normal body temperature, blood pressure, sugar levels, etc.). The body attempts to maintain internal homeostasis or balance in face of environmental stress. Cannon coined the phrase fight-or-flight to refer to the set of physiological processes evoked in response to stress.

Hans Selye (1856) was a Canadian endocrinologist expanded upon these ideas and created the foundations for modern conceptualizations of stress. Selye exposed laboratory rats to various extreme environmental stressors, including freezing, constant light, noise, and so on. He found that when a rat's homeostasis was pushed too much out of balance, the adaptational demands were to great and death often followed.

Selye also found that many environmental stressors evoked the same destabilizing pattern for many species of animals. He called this disruption *stress* or the *nonspecific response to demand*. The body process of attempting to adapt to severe environmental stressors progresses through three phases, which Seyle called the **general adaptation syndrome (GAS)**:

Alarm. This is the fight-or-flight response. The body becomes energized to adapt to stressor demands. To use an analogy, imagine someone triggers a fire alarm in a big building. At first, many fire trucks arrive in a wholesale generalized emergency response.

Resistance. If a serious stressor continues, the fight-or-flight response subsides. The body attempts to adapt more efficiently and directs resources to where they are most needed. Most of the "fire trucks" return home, and only those that are needed stay. But there is a cost. Resistance takes energy, and gradually leads to wear and tear, first on weak organs. Returning to the fire engine, imagine the fire cannot be put out (because of an underground pocket of gas or flammable coal). Fighters keep on fighting. When a truck is worn out or a fighter grows tired, replacements come in. As this continues over the days, the resources of the fire department dwindle, and the city budget experiences the strain.

Exhaustion. Eventually, as resources are depleted, the body begins to break down. Fewer resources are available for dealing with other problems like infection. Eventually death ensues.

Early pioneering work on stress focus on extreme environmental conditions (cold, heat, noise, light), perhaps because they are easy to quantify and study. Although the simple stimulus-response (stressor - arousal /distress) model researchers first used has now been replaced by more sophisticated models that recognize the importance of coping, thinking, and self-stressing, one important legacy continues. In people, and in laboratory rats, environmental stressors not only create stress, but they deplete adaptational resources that are important for dealing with other life stressors. As the body diverts energy to cope with extremes in temperature, less energy is available for finding food or safety. As more fire engines are sent to the fire emergency, fewer engines are available for fires elsewhere.

Environmental Stressors

Light

Too much light can be irritating, and a source of stress. But how much light is too much? First consider the type of light that illuminates your immediate environment.

Direct, bright light. Consider how brightly illuminated your immediate environment is. The ideal amount of illumination differs depending on the area. Detailed workmanship and careful reading of small print requires more light than general office work. General office work requires more light than retail store space. Hallways require relatively little light. Light is too bright if it washes out detail.

Reflected light. Light that bounces off objects, such as car windows, building glass, shiny floors, and mirrors, and then enters your viewing area can contribute to eyestrain and stress.

Glare. Glare is excessive light that bounces off what you are viewing. It is defined by the viewing angle, and the angle of light. For example, you may be reading a book directly under a spotlight. Light bounces directly off the page into your eyes, so you can't see the print. You shift the book to reduce the glare. Excessive glare can lead to eyestrain, headaches, and fatigue, partly because it triggers constant contraction of face muscles.

High-contrast light. Excessive contrast in the lighting of one's surroundings can cause eyestrain. For example, a brightly lit computer station, surrounded by very darkly lit bookcases and a black floor is a high-contrast and potentially stressful light environment. A bright computer monitor in a totally dark room is another example.

Temperature

Living and working in an environment that is either too hot or too cold is not only distracting – it is a source of environmental stress. Technically, when humidity is about 50% (a typical standard, lower in the winter), different situations call for different ideal temperatures. The Occupational Safety and Health Administration(2003) offers the following recommendations: Sedentary work is best at 70-75 degrees Fahrenheit. Working involving standing and doing light physical labor can be done at cooler temperatures, ideally 66 - 72 degrees. Manual labor calls for temperatures cooler than the ideal for light work.

In cooler temperatures, blood flows out of the hands, reducing manual dexterity. Severe loss of motor coordination and control can occur when temperatures drops below 55 degrees.

Air Quality

Poor air quality can be a source of stress or increase our vulnerability to other stressors. You are not at your best in a smoke-filled room. There are many types of indoor air pollution, including dust mites, pests such as bugs and rodents, pets, mold, secondhand smoke and nitrogen dioxide.

The effects of indoor air pollution may show up after a single exposure or several exposures. Some of the first effects include irritation of the eyes, nose, and throat, headaches, dizziness, and fatigue – some of the same symptoms associated with stress. Some immediate effects are similar to the effects of colds and viral diseases, so it can be difficult to identify the source. For this reason it is important to pay attention to when and where symptoms occur, and if the symptoms go away when one leaves a potentially polluted indoor setting.

Long-term effects of repeated exposure may include some respiratory diseases, heart diseases, and cancer (EPA, 1995).

The two most frequently recommended ways of treating indoor air pollution are (1) identifying and removing the source, and (2) increasing air ventilation, which is, the amount of outdoor air that enters a room or building. There is much wisdom to the common-sense advise, "Get rid of that smoking cigar, and open the windows!" In addition, air cleaning devices can be of some value; however, small, table-top models have little value. For recent reviews, see: www.consumerreports.org .

The Environmental Protection Agency (EPA, 2004) has a asthma home checklist which I recommend as a more general checklist of indoor air pollution. This same checklist (available on the internet) provides concrete and practical suggestions for reducing pollution.

Noise

Noise is in the ear of the irritated (just as beauty is in the eye of the beholder). That is, any sound you don't want to hear is noise to you. Noise is not always the same as sound volume, or the actual decibel level of sound. Sound volume can vary from 20 decibels in the quiet countryside, 50-70 decibels downtown, 90 or more decibels in factors or large dance parties, to over 120 decibels near a jet at takeoff. If you are used to the peaceful outdoors, downtown may seem to be very noisy. If you spend much time in teen dance parties, downtown may seem downright serene! Most aversive noise is secondhand noise, which like secondhand smoke, is created by others. Common sources of serious noise (which is both irritating and potentially damaging) include industrial plants, construction, and traffic (Noise Clearninghouse, 2003).

When can we say that noise is seriously loud? The Federal Highway Administration (FHWA, 1995) uses three criterial for evaluating the seriousness of noise:

1. Does the noise lead to hearing impairment?
2. Is the noise annoying or interfere with sleep or task performance?
3. Does the noise interfere with speech communication?

Too much high-volume noise can lead to various levels of hearing loss including difficulty hearing the telephone to trouble making out consonant sounds such a s *s, sh, ch, and th.* Hearing loss can also contribute to symptoms similar to those associated with stress, including problems concentrating, fatigue, low self-confidence, irritation, and impaired performance (Lercher, 1996; Rosenlund, et al. 2001; Van Kempen, et al., 2002).

In addition, noise and noise-related sleep loss can contribute to such stress-related symptoms as increased blood pressure, fatigue, depression, and impaired performance. It is not surprising that research has found environmental noise to be associated with increased anxiety, nausea, headaches, hostility, sexual impotency, interpersonal conflict, and even mental illness (Lercher, 1996; Nadakavukaren, 2000).

INDOOR POLLUTION CHECKLIST

POLLUTION SOURCE: DUST MITES

Triggers. Body parts and droppings
Where found: Highest levels found in mattresses and bedding. Also found in carpeting, curtains, and draperies, upholstered furniture, and stuffed toys. Dust mites are too small to be seen with the naked eye and are found in almost every home.

POLLUTION SOURCE: PESTS (BUGS, MICE)

Triggers. Cockroaches - Body parts, secretions, and droppings. Rodents - Hair, skin flakes, urine, and saliva.
Where found. Often found in areas with food and water such as kitchens, bathrooms, and basements.

POLLUTION SOURCE: WARM-BLOODED PETS (CATS, DOGS, ETC.)

Triggers. Skin flakes, urine, and saliva ("dander")
Where found. Throughout entire house, if allowed inside

POLLUTION SOURCE: MOLD

Triggers. Mold and mold spores which may begin growing indoors when they land on damp or wet surfaces. Where found. Often found in areas with excess moisture such as kitchens, bathrooms, and basements. There are many types of mold and they can be found in any climate.

SECONDHAND SMOKE

Trigger. Secondhand smoke - mixture of smoke from the burning end of a cigarette, pipe or cigar and the smoke exhaled by a smoker
Where found. Home or care where smoking is allowed.

NITROGEN DIOXIDE (COMBUSTION BY-PRODUCT)

Trigger. Nitrogen dioxide - an odorless gas that can irritate your eyes, nose, and throat and may cause shortness of breath.
Where found. Associated with gas cooking appliances, fireplaces, wood stoves, and unvented kerosene and gas space heaters.

EPA, 2004

CHAPTER 33
STRESS AT WORK: CAUSES AND COSTS

The National Institute for Occupational Safety and Health (NIOSH) is the Federal agency responsible for conducting research and making recommendations for the prevention of work-related illness and injury. As part of its mandate, NIOSH is directed by Congress to study the psychological aspects of occupational safety and health, including stress and work. NIOSH works with industry, labor, and universities to better understand the nature of stress at worry, its effects on worker safety and health, and ways of reducing workplace stress. This chapter presents material from NOISH (1999). Given its importance, it is presented in a form that you may freely copy, reprint, and distribute in any way you wish. You may wish to acquire and distribute copies of a *"Stress at Work,"* a free booklet from NIOSH (1999), that presents the information in this chapter.

Job stress comes in many forms. However, often different stressful types of work share the same stressful characteristics. Consider the following story.

Steve is waiting nervously in his doctor's office. For weeks he has been suffering from a variety of stress-related physical symptoms, including fatigue, stomach distress, and headaches. To make things work, his home life has suffered. Steve has become something of an angry tyrant at home, complaining and arguing with his wife and two children. And the grandparents have moved on and another child is on the way.

Steve's most frequent complaint is work. For the past five years he has been a customer complaint officer at a large downtown department store. He used to enjoy his job and looked forward to advancing to a managerial position. Every day had its challenges, calling for creative solutions. However, things have changed. Steve's store is downsizing, and the management is cutting corners. The first "efficiency steps" seemed minor. The cleaning staff was cut back and assigned to clean once a week

rather than once a day. The water cooler was removed. Extra workers were moved into Frank's office space and some had to double-up on desks. The workplace became noisy, dirty, and uncomfortable.

Soon it became clear that economizing and downsizing meant that no one's job was safe. As people left, others had to take over. Steve found himself doing the work of two or three people. His hours became unpredictable. Sometimes he worked evenings, sometimes early mornings. Steve hoped for some flexibility in scheduling hours. Even here he had to follow the rules rigidly given by his supervisors.

Steve used to enjoy socializing with his friends at work. Now many have left or there's no time. However, nearly everyone complains how the new management just doesn't listen. They feel stuck in something of a rat race, working hard just to keep up. Many feel there is no way out, and no future in a downsizing organization that is poorly run.

Steve's story is becoming increasingly common. Job stress can become a serious and costly problem. Perhaps one-fourth of workers see their jobs as their number one life stressor employees (Northwestern National Life Insurance Company, 1992). Three-fourths of employees believe the worker has more on-the-job stress than a generation ago (Princeton Survey Research Associates, 1997). Problems at work are more strongly associated with health complaints than are any other life stressor – more so than even financial problems or family problems (St. Paul Fire and Marine Insurance Co., 1992).

What is Job Stress?

Job stress can be defined as the harmful physical and emotional responses that occur when the *requirements of the job do not meet the capabilities, resources, or needs of the workers.* In other words it is problem of job / worker fit and can lead to poor health and injury.

Job stress is not the same as challenge. Challenge energizes and motivates us to learn new skills and mater our jobs. When a challenge is met, we're relaxed and satisfied. Thus challenge is an important part of heathy and productive work. Indeed, a little bit of job stress is good for you.

In our example of Steve, we see how a possibly challenging job can become a source of stress, possibly leading to illness, frustration, and poor performance.

Causes of Job Stress

There are two causes of job stress: work conditions and worker characteristics. **Stressful working conditions** (job stressors such as too much work, little control, noisy environments) can directly influence safety and health. **Individual and situational factors** may intensity or weaken the effects. Steve's physical complains, as well as his busy family life, are individual and situational factors that can aggravate the impact of stressful that working conditions.

The NOISH model of job stress is summarized in this widely-cited illustration, presented here.

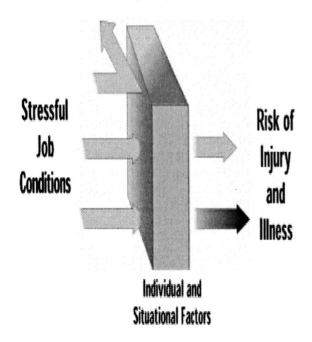

Stressful Job Conditions

Do you work under stressful conditions? NIOSH has summarized six things to look for:

1. *The Design of Work Tasks*
2. *Management Style*
3. *Interpersonal Relationships*
4. *Work Roles*
5. *Career Concerns*
6. *Environmental Conditions*

The Design of Tasks

- ❏ Heavy workload
- ❏ Infrequent rest breaks
- ❏ Long work hours and shift work
- ❏ Hectic / routine tasks with little meaning
- ❏ Work that underutilizes your skills
- ❏ Work that provides little sense of control

Example: Steve has to do the work of several people, with few reset breaks. Often he works long hours, and feel s little control over his hours.

Management Style

- ❏ Lack of participation by workers in decision-making
- ❏ Poor communication in the organization
- ❏ Lack of family-friendly policies

Example: Steve and his coworkers do not take part in creating work schedules. Assignments come down from supervisors without discussion.

Interpersonal Relationships

- ❏ Poor social environment
- ❏ Lack of support or help from coworkers
- ❏ Lack of support or help from supervisors

Example: Steve's workload is so hectic that he has little chance to socialize, or seek help from others.

Work Roles

- ❏ Conflicting or uncertain job expectations
- ❏ Too much responsibility
- ❏ Too many "hats to wear"

Example: As Steve's workplace downsizes, he takes on uncertain jobs from others. Often he does two jobs at once.

Career Concerns

- ❏ Job insecurity
- ❏ Lack of opportunity for growth, advancement, or promotion
- ❏ Rapid changes for which workers are unprepared

Example: Steve and his coworkers worry about their future in the organization. Things change without warning.

Environmental Conditions

- ❏ Unpleasant or dangerous physical conditions such as crowding, noise, air pollution, or ergonomic problems.

Example: Steve's work space has deteriorated and is uncomfortable and possibly even unsafe.

Feedback and Communication

Many of these problems are made worse by poor feedback and communication. Often, simply letting workers know the facts can reduce uncertainty and a sense of helpless. Knowing what's really going on also gives workers the best opportunity to consider realistic coping options. Signs of poor feedback and communication include:

- ❏ Not receiving clear, specific, and immediate constructive feedback when you make a mistake or can do something better.
- ❏ Not receiving clear, specific, and immediate praise and positive feedback when you have done something right or completed a job particularly well.

- ❏ Not being informed of the full extent of challenges or problems that may be present at work.

Individual and Situational Factors

NIOSH provides three examples of individual and situational factors that can help to reduce the effects of stressful working conditions:

- Balance between work and family or personal life
- A support network of friends and coworkers
- A relaxed and positive outlook.

To these I believe it is important to add maintaining a healthy lifestyle, including:

- Getting enough sleep
- Eating properly
- Getting enough exercise
- Conscientiously taking care of medical problems (taking medications, following doctor's orders.)

However, the perspective of this book personal coping skills, specifically the basic skills of:

- ❏ Learning relaxation and meditation / mindfulness (six relaxation access skills)
- ❏ Applying effective problem-solving skills
- ❏ Thinking rationally and realistically

To this we can add the following major application skills:

- ❏ Desensitization and relapse-prevention
- ❏ Assertiveness
- ❏ Dealing with shyness
- ❏ Managing anger and aggression

The Costs and Warning Signs of Job Stress: Illness and Productivity Loss

NIOSH identifies the following early warning signs of job stress:

- Headache
- Sleep disturbances
- Difficulty in concentrating
- Short temper
- Upset stomach
- Job dissatisfaction
- Low morale

In addition, we add high scores on the Stress Symptoms Scale presented earlier.

Low morale, health and job complaints, and employee turnover often provide the first signs of job stress. But sometimes there are no clues, especially if employees are fearful of losing their jobs. Lack of obvious or widespread signs is not a good reason to dismiss concerns about job stress or minimize the importance of a prevention program.

Left unchecked, job stress can impact health and productivity, contributing to:

- **Cardiovascular disease**. Many studies suggest that psychologically demanding jobs that allow employees little control over the work process increase the risk of cardiovascular disease.

- **Musculoskeletal disorders**. On the basis of research by NIOSH and many other organizations, it is widely believed that job stress increases the risk for development of back and upper-extremity Musculoskeletal disorders.

- **Psychological disorders**. Several studies suggest that differences in rates of mental health problems (such a depression and burnout) for various occupations are due partly to differences in job stress levels. (Economic and lifestyle differences between occupations may also contribute to some of these problems.)

- **Suicide, cancers, ulcers, and impaired immune function**. Some studies suggest a relationship between stressful working conditions and these health problems. However, more research is needed.

- **Workplace injury**. Although more study is needed, there is a growing concern that stressful working conditions interfere with safe work practices and set the stage for injuries at work.

- **Productivity loss**. Some employers assume that stressful working conditions are a necessary evil – that companies must turn up the pressure on workers and set aside health concerns to remain productive and profitable in today's economy. But research findings challenge this belief. Studies show that stressful working conditions are actually associated with increased **absenteeism, tardiness, and intentions by workers to quit their jobs** – all of which have a negative effect on the bottom line.

CHAPTER 34
PREVENTING STRESS AT WORK

Job stress management focuses on individual/situational problems and stressful job conditions. The National Institute for Occupational Safety and Health NIOSH (1999) concludes that partial approaches aren't enough. For example, often businesses use "stress workshop" seminars that offer information about stress. Various approaches to relaxation, especially yoga and time management, are also popular. But such strategies have limited effectiveness. One needs to include other approaches to individual/situational stress management as well modifying stressful job conditions through organizational change. NIOSH recommends that **a combination of organizational change and [individual/situational] stress management is often the most useful approach to preventing stress at work.**

This book covers the basic approaches to individual / situational stress management. A wide range of organizational changes may also be considered. This chapter presents material offered by NIOSH (1999).

Stress Management Target Goals

First, consider the following specific target goals (adapted from Sauter, Murphy, & Hurrell, 1990)

❑ Recognition of employees for good work performance
❑ Increase opportunities for career development
❑ Cultivate an organizational culture that values the individual worker
❑ Ensure consistency between management actions and stated organizational values.
❑ Ensure that the workload is in line with workers' capabilities and resources
❑ Design jobs to provide meaning, stimulation, and opportunities for workers to use their skills.

❑ Clearly define workers roles and responsibilities
❑ Give workers opportunities to participate in decisions and actions affecting their jobs.
❑ Improve communications – reduce uncertainty about career development and future employment prospects
❑ Provide opportunities for social interaction among workers
❑ Establish work schedules that are compatible with demands and responsibilities outside the job.

The NIOSH Program for Minimizing Stressful Job Conditions

This chapter presents a three-step program recommended by NIOSH. In order for this program to work, organizations must first be prepared.

Before Attempting Job Stress Management

❑ Provide a basic introduction on stress, its causes and costs, and how it can be controlled. Copies of the NIOSH (1999) publication "Stress at Work" may be distributed and discussed at a workshop
❑ Meet with top management, explain the program, and seek their support. Management must understand and sincerely support whatever stress management program is initiated.
❑ Involve employees at all phases of the program.
❑ Know what you are doing. Study this book. For others working with you, introduce in-house training for workers who plan to participate as assistants.

It can be particularly useful to have workers and managers work together in task-oriented problem-solving and brainstorming sessions (see Chapters 14 and 15). Such participation is effective and works by making use of the direct experience and differences in perspective of workers and managers.

When creating such work groups, make sure that they comply with current labor laws. The National Labor Relations Act may limit the form and structure of employee involvement in worker-management teams or groups. Employers should seek legal assistance if they are unsure of their responsibilities or obligations under the National Labor Relations Act.

The 3-Step NIOSH Stress Prevention Program

Step 1 - Identify the problem. The best method to explore the scope and source of a suspected stress problem in an organization depends partly on the size of the organization and the available resources. Group discussions among managers, labor representatives, and employees can provide rich sources of information. Discussions may be all that is needed to find and fix problems in a small company. In a larger organization, such discussions can be used to help design formal surveys for gathering input about stressful job conditions from large numbers of employees.

Regardless of the method used to collect data, information should be obtained about employee perceptions of their job conditions and perceived levels of stress, health, and satisfaction. The list of job conditions that may lead to stress and the warning signs and effects of stress (Chapters 2 and 3) provided starting points for deciding what information to collect. You may consider using the Stress Test at the end of Chapter 3. I offer a possible additional inventory at the end of this chapter.

Objective measures such as absenteeism, illness and turnover rates, or performance problems can also be examined to gauge the presence and scope of job stress. However, these measure are only rough indicators of job stress.

Data from discussions, surveys, and other sources should be summarized and analyzed to answer questions about the location of a stress problem and job conditions that may be responsible – for example, are problems present throughout the organization or confined to single department or specific jobs. In summary:

- Hold group discussions with employees
- Design and employee survey (perhaps using the instruments at the end of this chapter and in Chapter 3)

- Measure employee perceptions of job conditions, stress, health, and satisfaction
- Collect objective data
- Analyze data to identify problem locations and stressful job conditions.

Step 2 – Design and implement interventions. Once the sources of stress at work have been identified and the scope of the problem is understood, the stage is set for design and implementation of an intervention strategy.

In small organizations, the informal discussions that helped identify stress problems may also produce fruitful ideas for prevention. In large organizations a more formal process may be needed. Frequently, a team is asked to develop recommendations based on analysis of data from Step 1 and consultation with outside experts.

Certain problems, such as a hostile work environment, may be pervasive in the organization and require company-wide interventions.. Other problems such as excessive workload may exist only in some departments and thus require more narrow solutions such as redesign of the way a job is performed. Still other problems may be specific to certain employees and resistant to any kind of organizational change, calling instead for stress management or employee assistance interventions. Some interventions might be implemented rapidly (e.g, improved communication, individual stress management training), but others may require additional time to put into pace (e.g., redesign of a manufacturing process).

Before any intervention occurs, employees should be informed about actions that will be taken and when they will a occur. A kick-off event, such as an all-hands meeting, is often useful for this purpose. To summarize:

- Target the source of stress for change
- Propose and prioritize intervention strategies
- Communicate planned interventions to employees
- Implement interventions.

Step 3 - Evaluate the interventions. Evaluation is an essential step in the intervention process. Evaluation is necessary to determine whether the intervention is producing desired effects and whether changes in direction are needed.

Time frames for evaluating interventions should be established. Interventions involving organizational change should receive both short-

and long-term scrutiny. Short-term evaluations might be done quarterly to provide an early indication of program effectiveness or possible need for redirection. Many interventions produce initial effects that do not persist. Long-term evaluations are often conducted annually and are necessary to determine whether interventions produce lasting effects.

Evaluations should focus on the same types of information collected during the problem identification phase of the intervention, including information from employees about working conditions, levels of perceived stress, health problems, and satisfaction. Employee perceptions are usually the most sensitive measure of stressful working conditions and often provide the first indication of intervention effectiveness. Adding objective measures such as absenteeism and health care costs may also be useful. However, the effects of job stress interventions on such measures tend to be less clear-cut and can take a long time to appear. The job stress process does not end with evaluation. Rather, job stress prevention should be seen as a continuous process that uses evaluation data to refine or redirect the intervention strategy. To summarize:

- Conduct both short- and long-term evaluations
- Measure employee perceptions of job conditions, stress, health, and satisfaction.
- Include objective measures.
- Refine the intervention strategy.

What Some Organizations have Done Illustrations from NIOSH

A Small Service Organization

A department head in a small public service organization sensed an escalating level of tension and deteriorating morale among her staff. Job dissatisfaction and health symptoms such as headaches also seemed to be on the rise. Suspecting that stress was a developing problem in the department, she decided to hold a series of all-hands meetings with employees in the different work units of the department to explore this concern further. These meetings could best be described as brainstorming sessions where individual employees freely expressed their views about the scope and sources of stress in their units and the measures that might be implemented to bring the problem under control.

Using the information collected in these meetings with middle managers, she concluded that a serious problem probably existed and that quick action was needed. Because

she was relatively unfamiliar with the job stress field, she decided to seek help from a faculty member at a local university who taught courses on job stress and organizational behavior.

After reviewing the information collected at the brainstorming sessions, they decided it would be useful for the faculty member to conduct informal classes to raise awareness about job stress — it causes, effects, and prevention — for all workers and managers in the department. It was also decided that as survey would be useful to obtain a more reliable picture of problematic job conditions and stress-related health complaints in the department. The faculty member used information from the meetings with workers and managers to design the survey. The faculty member was also involved in the distribution and collection of the anonymous survey to ensure that workers felt free to respond honestly and openly about what was bothering the. He then helped the department head analyze and interpret the data.

Analysis f the survey data suggested that three types of job conditions were linked to stress complaints among the workers:

- *Unrealistic deadlines*
- *Low levels of support form supervisors*
- *Lack of worker involvement in decision-making.*

Having pinpointed these problems, the department head developed and prioritized a list of corrective measures for implementation. Examples of these actions included (1) greater participation of employees in work scheduling to reduce unrealistic deadlines and (2) more frequent meetings between workers and managers to keep supervisors and workers updated on developing problems.

A Large Manufacturing Company

Although no widespread signs of stress were evident at work, the corporate medical director of a large manufacturing company thought it would be useful to establish a stress prevention program as a proactive measure. As a first step he discussed this concept with senior management and with union leaders. Together, they decided to organize a labor-management team to develop the program. The team comprised representatives from labor, the medical / employee assistance department, the human resource department, and an outside human resources consulting firm. The consulting fir provided technical advice about program design, implementation, and evaluation. Financial resources for the team and program came from senior management, who made it clear that the supported this activity. The team designed a two-part program. One part focused on management practices and working conditions that could lead to stress. The second part focused on individual health and well-being.

To begin the part of the program dealing with management practices and job conditions, the team worked with the consulting firm to add new questions about job stress to the company's existing employee opinion survey. The survey data were used by the team to identify stressful working conditions and to suggest changes at the work group and / or organizational level. The employee health and well-being part of the program consisted of 12 weekly training sessions. During these sessions, workers and managers learned about common sources and effects of stress at work, and about self-protection strategies such as relaxation methods and improved health behaviors. The training sessions were offered during both work and nonwork hours.

The team followed up with quarterly surveys of working conditions and stress symptoms to closely monitor the effectiveness of this two-part program.

THE JOB STRESS INVENTORY

Consider your present job (or if unemployed, your most recent job). Please rate the extent to which each of the following statements fits you. Please rate each statement, using the following key:

O	①	②	③
DOESN'T FIT ME AT ALL	FITS ME A LITTLE	FITS ME MODERATELY	FITS ME VERY WELL

PART 1: PERSONAL SYMPTOMS

O ① ② ③   1.   I am dissatisfied with my job
O ① ② ③   2.   I have low morale at work
O ① ② ③   3.   I have symptoms which seem to be related to job stress.
O ① ② ③   4.   I have an illness which job stress seems to be making worse.
O ① ② ③   5   I find myself taking a lot of "mental health holidays" or not showing up for work.
O ① ② ③   6.   I find it hard to get myself "psyched up" or motivated for work, and often arrive at work late
O ① ② ③   7.   I frequently think about quitting my job

PART II: SOURCES OF JOB STRESS

Design of Work Tasks

O ① ② ③   1.   My workload is too heavy
O ① ② ③   2.   I need more rest breaks at work
O ① ② ③   3.   My work day is too long
O ① ② ③   4.   I'm having trouble coping with shift work (sometimes working nights, sometimes days)
O ① ② ③   5.   Things are too hectic at work
O ① ② ③   6.   I find my job too routine with little inherent meaning
O ① ② ③   7.   My job underutilizes my skills
O ① ② ③   8.   My job gives me little sense of control; I have little "say" about things

Management style

O ① ② ③   1.   Workers do not participate enough in decision-making
O ① ② ③   2.   There is poor communication at work. I don't know what's going on or what's expected.
O ① ② ③   3.   This job lacks family-friendly policies

Interpersonal relationships

O ① ② ③   1.   Where I work does not provide a friendly or comfortable social environment.
O ① ② ③   2.   I do not get enough support or help from coworkers
O ① ② ③   3.   I do not get enough support or help from supervisors

Work roles

O ① ② ③   1.   I have to deal with conflicting or uncertain job expectations
O ① ② ③   2.   I am burdened with too much responsibility
O ① ② ③   3.   I have many "hats to wear" at work

Career concerns

O ① ② ③   1.   I feel I have to worry too much about job insecurity
O ① ② ③   2.   My job has a lack of opportunity for growth, advancement, or promotion
O ① ② ③   3.   I am confronted with rapid changes for which workers are unprepared

Environmental conditions

O ① ② ③   1.   There are unpleasant or dangerous physical conditions such as crowding, noise, or air pollution
O ① ② ③   2.   The equipment I work with, including chairs, desks, computers, etc., are uncomfortable and poorly designed.

Feedback

O ① ② ③   1.   I do not get clear, specific, and immediate constructive feedback when I make a mistake or could do better.
O ① ② ③   2.   I do not get clear, specific, and immediate praise and positive feedback when I do something right or well.
O ① ② ③   3.   I am not informed of the full extent of challenges or problems that may be present at work.

PART III: I THINK THIS JOB NEEDS . . .

○ ① ② ③   1. More recognition of employees for good work performance
○ ① ② ③   2. More opportunities for career development
○ ① ② ③   3. More of a culture that values the individual worker
○ ① ② ③   4. More consistency between management actions and stated
                       organizational values.
○ ① ② ③   5. Workload that is in line with workers' capabilities and resources
○ ① ② ③   6. Work that is meaningful, stimulating, and gives me a chance to
                       use my skills
○ ① ② ③   7. A clear definition of my roles and responsibilities
○ ① ② ③   8. More opportunities to participate in decisions and actions
                       affecting my job
○ ① ② ③   9. Improved communications
○ ① ② ③ 10. Reduced uncertainty about career development and future
                       employment prospects
○ ① ② ③ 11. More opportunities for social interaction among workers
○ ① ② ③ 12. Work schedules that are compatible with demands and
                       responsibilities outside the job.

Adapted from: National Institute for Occupational Safety and Health (NOISH; 1999). *Stress at work.* (DHHS Publication No. 99-101). Washington, DC: US Government Printing Office.

Note: Examples in this chapter are based on adaptations of actual situations. For other examples of job stress interventions, see the Conditions of Work Digest, Vol 11/2, pp. 139-275. This publication may be obtained by contacting the ILO Publications Center at P.O. Box 753, Waldorf, MD 20604 (Telephone: 301-638-3152). Or call NIOSH at 1-800-35-NIOSH.

CHAPTER 35
CRISES AND CATASTROPHES

In times of war, crisis, and terrorist attack and threat, we are often confronted with stressors that are unusually severe and traumatic. Even in more ordinary times, people encounter crises and catastrophes. In this chapter we consider traumatic stressors, defined as events outside the realm of ordinary experience associated with feelings intense fear, helplessness, or horror. Unfortunately, many events fall into this category. (Smith, 2001):

Examples of Crises and Catastrophes

Deliberate Human Activities

- Wartime violence, destruction, injury, and death
- Terrorist attack
- Breakdown of social infrastructure (mail delivery system; health system; air transportation; communication network; energy, food, and water resources)
- Bombing
- Riot
- Military combat
- Sexual assault
- Sexual abuse
- Physical attack
- Serious Physical abuse
- Robbery
- Mugging
- Kidnaping
- Being taken hostage
- Torture
- Involuntary incarceration
- Suicide/death

Unintentional Human (accidents, technological disaster)

- Serious automobile accident
- Serious industrial accident
- Serious sports / recreational accident
- Breakdown of social infrastructure (mail delivery system, health system, air transportation, communication network) -- if not due to terrorist attack
- Nuclear power plant disaster
- Surgical damage to body
- Fires and explosions
- Plane crash
- Train wreck
- Boating accident/shipwreck
- Building/ major structure collapse

Acts of Nature / Natural Disaster

- Earthquake
- Flood
- Global warming
- Epidemic / plague (not human origin)
- Meteor/Comet catastrophe
- Hurricane/tornado
- Heat wave
- Severe snow/rain
- Avalanche/mudslide
- Brush fire
- Famine
- Sinkholes
- Animal (wild dog/cat, bear) attack
- Severe illness or medical incident (heart attack)
- Death of loved one

One need not be a direct victim to experience the impact of crises and catastrophes; traumatic events can be witnessed or learned about through word of mouth, television, radio, the internet, or the print media.

(American Psychiatric Association, Diagnostic and Statistical Manual of Mental Disorders, 4th ed. text revision, 2000; Schiraldi, 2000; Smith, 2001)

Health professionals have a name for the reactions we often have when confronting a trauma – Acute Stress Disorder. We are likely to experience Acute Stress Disorders after an even that evokes feelings of intense fear, helplessness, or horror. One of the first steps in coping with such trauma is to recognize and understand the symptoms that can arise. These symptoms are often a normal response to an abnormal situation, and can pass within a month or so. If they are exceptionally severe (interfering with work or school) and persist more than a month, then professional help is required.

Avoidance

After a severe trauma, it is understand that a victim might want to avoid all memories and reminders of the event. This can involve avoiding places related to or similar to where the event occurred, or avoiding conversations or people related to the trauma. You might not want to think about the event at all, and put it out of mind.

Dissociation

Sometimes victims of trauma avoid things without knowing it. Such unconscious avoidance is called dissociation. One can dissociate in several ways.

Psychic (or "psychological") numbing. This has nothing to do with "psychics"or the occult. "Psychic numbing" is a state in which you feel numb, detached, uninvolved in life. You may have difficulty loving, crying, laughing, caring, or even feeling anger. You may no longer find fun and pleasure in activities you used to like. Numbing is a psychological defense mechanism in which one tunes out all feelings in order to "tune out" painful feelings related to a trauma.

Reduced awareness of surroundings. You simply might not notice or respond to other people or events. People might say you seem to be , "in a daze," "spaced out" or "in one's own private world." As with numbing, this is a way to tune out traumatic pain. If you are less aware of everything, you are less aware of memories and reminders of your trauma.

Derealization. This strange psychiatric term is hard to describe. Have you ever seen a long, engaging, and strange movie, walked into the daylight sun, and found that things and people seemed different – perhaps more vivid, perhaps unfamiliar, strange, unreal, dreamlike, or mechanical. Your perception of what's real has been slightly altered, and you experience derealization. Maybe you overslept, and when waking up felt a little confused. You may have wondered, "What day is this? What time is it?" Again, you have tasted a bit of derealization, in that parts of the normal ordinary world seem different.   And perhaps you have witnessed a friend having a mildly distressing reaction to marijuana or some other drug. He or she may say they feel detached from their familiar world. Things might seem like they are not real, or not really happening. They may feel like they are a stranger or an outsider, even in familiar places. Maybe events seem speeded or slowed down. Again, one's reality has been altered, and one is experiencing a type of derealization. Most people have had mild experiences of derealization from time to time. Derealization may be both an attempt

to distance oneself from a trauma and a secondary effect of numbing and reduced awareness.

Depersonalization. Here's another psychiatric term. Depersonalization is a little like derealization, except that your experience of your body or self is distorted.   Examples include "out of body experiences" in which one has the experience of being separated from one's body, perhaps looking down from above or across the room, or watching a movie of oneself. The body might seem like it's split into parts, or one part of the body might feel numb, warm, or cold.   Depersonalization, like derealization, serves to distance oneself from trauma.

Amnesia. Amnesia is both a psychiatric term and a word in everyday language. When you experience amnesia, you simply can't remember something. This is common in times of stress. You often read or hear of people who can't remember details of a traumatic crime, attack, or accident. Often, memory returns.

Re-experiencing the Trauma

Sometimes instead of avoiding and dissociating from reminders of a trauma, one experiences just the opposite, re-experiencing a trauma. There are many ways a crisis or catastrophe can stick in your mind, including: fantasies about the trauma, worrisome thoughts, and nightmares.

You may experience flashbacks in which the trauma is re-experienced or "replayed" mentally. Flashbacks are predominantly visual, and can be so vivid that you think you are reliving an event. They can be triggered by lack of sleep, fatigue, stress arousal, drugs, or deep relaxation.

Also, you may find that stimuli that remind you of the trauma creates distress. These can include people who look like or wear the same clothes as those involved in the trauma, places, objects, weather conditions, and so on. Sometimes you may be confronted with such a reminder quite unexpectedly, or even distort what you are seeing or hearing so they become trauma reminders. Someone who in fact may look very little like a lost loved one, may suddenly resemble the loved one.

An fundamental part of all stress is arousal / distress. Arousal / distress can be exaggerated in victims of crisis or catastrophe.   There are many symptoms

- *Difficulty sleeping*
- *Irritability, emotional outbursts, arguing, intense criticizing, impatience*
- *Overactive startle response*
- *Extreme restlessness, including fidgeting and pacing*
- *Hypersensitivity and being on guard*
- *Feeling constantly fearful and vulnerable*
- *Fear that the traumatic event may repeat itself, "fear of repetition":*
- *Taking extreme measures to protect oneself (having several weapons)*
- *Being overprotective or overcontrolling of loved one*

What's going on?

An Acute Stress Reaction is a serious response to trauma. It can take time to recover. Avoidance, dissociation, and re-experiencing the trauma can be seen as part of a process of **working through** the trauma (Horowitz, 1982). One's first reaction may be an intense emotional outcry, such as fainting, weeping, or panic. Physical and mental arousal may increase, potentially disrupting the working through process. When this happens, it can be very helpful to share your feelings with someone you trust.

The real "work" of working through often involves a two-part process in which one cycles between avoidance/dissociation and re-experiencing the trauma. One withdraws, approaches, withdraws, and then again approaches the trauma, reminders of the trauma, feelings associated with the trauma, and ramifications of the trauma. What is important to recognize is alternating phases of approach and withdrawal helps one deal with manageable pieces of a crisis. Put differently, a terrorist attack, disaster, loss of a loved one, or illness may be too big to deal with at once. For example, after losing one's house to a fire one might have to deal with the emotions of fear, rage, and depression as well as the tasks of finding new housing, dealing the feelings of family and loved ones, and so on. The phases of working through enable you to deal with pieces of the trauma in manageable doses, one at a time, and then withdraw to recover and regroup. When this happens, symptoms of re-experiencing a trauma help us take on a piece of a trauma; whereas withdrawal and dissociation are ways of taking a break.

Coping with and Resolving a Crisis or Catastrophe

If you seem to be stuck at any part of this working through process, or things are not getting better after a month, seek professional help. Generally, coping with crisis and catastrophe has short-term and long-term goals. The short-term goals are to remove any threat or danger to life, health, or well-being. Longer-term goals involve

1. To accept the crisis or catastrophe. It happened and can't be undone.
2. To learn to put the event aside the event so it is no longer a pressing concern, and
3. To go on coping and live a full a satisfying life.

Many of the techniques and strategies in this book can be very useful in dealing with a crisis or catastrophe. A trauma can be an excellent opportunity to learn and apply new ways of coping.

CHAPTER 34 EXERCISES

1. Crises and catastrophes in the news.

Go to the iInternet and search for articles that describe a genuine crisis and catastrophe, and how people reacted. Find examples of avoidance, dissociation, and re-experiencing the trauma. How did people cope and resolve the event? Did they use any of the approaches in this book?

2. A personal trauma

For some people, this can be a difficult exercise. Everyone has had the misfortune of having something very bad happen to them. What crisis or catastrophe have you experienced in your past? I recommend selecting one that is safely over, and one from which you have recovered.

- Describe the details of this crisis or catastrophe. What happened?

- Describe any symptoms of avoidance/dissociation as well as re-experiencing the trauma.

- Finally, describe what you thought and did to cope with and resolve the crisis or catastrophe. Did you use any of the approaches to stress management in this book?

PART VII
YOUR STRESS DIARY

YOUR STRESS MANAGEMENT DIARY: INSTRUCTIONS

Your Stress Management Diary gives you a chance to apply the concepts and tools in this book. At the end of every day fill out a diary page. In your diary select that day's most significant stressor. It is important that you avoid whining or complaining about a laundry list of problems ("everything went wrong. I felt so messed up"). Pick a specific example of stress for that day.

Every five days your diary has a special page for "Stress Management Review." On this page you think about the past days and what you have learned.

As you proceed through this book you will learn many new terms and techniques. When you see an illustration of a term in your life, note it in your diary. Report your successes and non-successes with the techniques mentioned in the book. Also, describe new techniques and strategies that you may have invented on your own.

FIRST, MAKE COPIES OF THE DIARY PAGE AND STRESS MANAGEMENT REVIEW PAGE.

DIARY EXAMPLE PAGES

TODAY'S DATE: **November 8, Monday**
TODAY'S MOST SIGNIFICANT STRESSOR INCIDENT

I missed my bus today and was late for class. The instructor gave me a strange look

FEELINGS AND SYMPTOMS OF AROUSAL / DISTRESS

I felt guilty and was very anxious.

WHAT HAPPENED? DESCRIBE WHAT YOU DID THAT MADE THINGS BETTER OR WORSE
✔ Where were you?   ✔ When did this happen? ✔ Who was involved? ✔ What happened?

I was in my bedroom and my alarm clock didn't go off. My dog woke me up. I then decided to take another few minutes of sleep and actually slept another hour. Eventually I woke up and realized that I was really late. I looked out of the window. The bus was just driving away. I knew I would be late. I waited for the next bus, and arrived at class 30 minutes late. I snuck in the back, but everyone turned around and stared at me. I felt awful!

EARLIEST WARNING SIGN THAT YOU MIGHT HAVE A PROBLEM

When my dog woke me up, I should have done something then and there. That would have helped a lot.

CONSEQUENCES

I was late to class and felt awful.

TODAY'S DATE: **November 9, Tuesday**

TODAY'S MOST SIGNIFICANT STRESSOR INCIDENT

I had an argument with my girlfriend.

FEELINGS AND SYMPTOMS OF AROUSAL / DISTRESS

She made me very angry and my stomach got upset.

WHAT HAPPENED? DESCRIBE WHAT YOU DID THAT MADE THINGS BETTER OR WORSE
✔ Where were you? ✔ When did this happen? ✔ Who was involved? ✔ What happened?

My girlfriend and I were walking down the street and she was taking her time adjusting her hair. It was Saturday and I wanted to get home quickly to watch the game. I started walking a little faster, and she kept walking too slowly. Finally, I got irritated and yelled, "hey, hurry up! I don't have all day!" She started yelling at me for being so selfish.

EARLIEST WARNING SIGN THAT YOU MIGHT HAVE A PROBLEM

When I noticed I was walking faster. That should have told me I felt in a hurry and should say something polite about it.

CONSEQUENCES

I got angry and upset at my girlfriend, and she got upset with me. We both started blowing things out of proportion.

TODAY'S DATE: **November 10, Wednesday**

TODAY'S MOST SIGNIFICANT STRESSOR INCIDENT

I borrowed my brother's car, ran a stop sign, and got caught by the police!

FEELINGS AND SYMPTOMS OF AROUSAL / DISTRESS

I was really afraid I was going to go to jail. This is the first time this has happened to me. My mind went blank I got so upset!

WHAT HAPPENED? DESCRIBE WHAT YOU DID THAT MADE THINGS BETTER OR WORSE
✔ Where were you? ✔ When did this happen? ✔ Who was involved? ✔ What happened?

It was early evening, about 7 PM and I was driving to the grocery store. I was driving down a quiet side street and there was no one around. I started thinking about the groceries I had to get and ran a stop sign. Suddenly, a cop car drove up behind me. I got out of my car and started to explain. She gave me a ticket. I was so upset I couldn't think. My mind went blank when she asked for my driver's licence. She must have thought I was really drunk!

EARLIEST WARNING SIGN THAT YOU MIGHT HAVE A PROBLEM

The moment I saw the cop behind me I might have tried to calm myself down. I could have taken some deep breaths and said to myself, "This is not the end of the world."

CONSEQUENCES

My mind went blank and I was upset the rest of the night

STRESS MANAGEMENT REVIEW

CHAPTERS COVERED: 1, 2, 3, 4

SUMMARIZE THE KEY POINTS YOU LEARNED FROM YOUR TEXT.

Stressors and what makes them bad.
The fight or flight response.
How the fight or flight response can mess us up.
How we make stress worse for ourselves.

EXAMPLES, ILLUSTRATIONS, OR APPLICATIONS OF THESE POINTS YOU EXPERIENCED THIS WEEK?

I had several stressors this week - late for class, the cop. They were all mild stressors. The worst thing about them was that they were unwanted.

I really felt the fight or flight response, especially anxiety when I was late for class and fear when the cop stopped me.

I self-stressed with my negative thinking.

NEW COPING STRATEGIES YOU USED THIS WEEK.. DESCRIBE COPING STRATEGIES YOU MIGHT HAVE TRIED.

When caught by the cop, I could have taken some breaths and "talked myself down" so I wouldn't be upset all night.

DIARY PAGE

TODAY'S DATE:

TODAY'S MOST SIGNIFICANT STRESSOR INCIDENT

FEELINGS AND SYMPTOMS OF AROUSAL / DISTRESS

WHAT HAPPENED? DESCRIBE WHAT YOU DID THAT MADE THINGS BETTER OR WORSE
✔ Where were you? ✔ When did this happen? ✔ Who was involved? ✔ What happened?

EARLIEST WARNING SIGN THAT YOU MIGHT HAVE A PROBLEM

CONSEQUENCES

STRESS MANAGEMENT REVIEW

CHAPTERS COVERED:

SUMMARIZE THE KEY POINTS YOU LEARNED FROM YOUR TEXT.

EXAMPLES, ILLUSTRATIONS, OR APPLICATIONS OF THESE POINTS YOU EXPERIENCED THIS WEEK?

NEW COPING STRATEGIES YOU USED THIS WEEK.. DESCRIBE COPING STRATEGIES YOU MIGHT HAVE TRIED.

REFERENCES

Alberti, R. E. & Emmons, Emmons, M. L. (1982). *Your perfect right.* San Luis Obispo, CA: Impact Publishers

American College of Sports Medicine (1998). AHA/ACSM joint statement: recommendations for cardiovascular screening, staffing, and emergency policies at health fitness facilities. *Medicine and science in sports and exercise, 30,* 1-19.

American Psychiatric Association (2000). *Diagnostic and statistical manual of mental disorders (4th ed., text revision).* Washington, DC: American Psychiatric Association.

Antony, M. M. & Swinson, R. P. (2000). *The shyness and social anxiety workbook.* Oakland, CA: New Harbinger.

Bower, S. A., & Bower, G. H. (1991). *Asserting yourself.* Cambridge, MA: Perseus Books.

Beck, A. T. (1993). *Cognitive therapy and the emotional disorders.* New York: American Library Trade.

Blonna, R. (2005). *Coping with stress in a changing world.* New York: McGraw-Hill

Borkovec, T. D. (1985). What's the use of worrying. *Psychology Today, 19,* 59-64.

Borkovec, T. D., Wilkinson, L., Folensbee, R. & Lerman, C. (1983). Stimulus control applications to the treatment of worry. *Behavior Research and Therapy, 21,* 247-251.

Burns, D. D. (1990). *The feeling good handbook.* New York: Plume

Cannon, W. B. (1929). *Bodily changes in pain, hunger, fear, and rage.* New York: Appleton.

Cannon, W. B. (1932). *The wisdom of the body.* New York: W. W. Norton

Curran, J. P., Wallander, J. L. & Farrell, A. D. (1985). Heterosocial skills training in L. L'Abate & M. A. Milan (Eds.) *Handbook of social skills training and research* (pp. 136-169). New York: Wiley.

Cautela, J. R. & Wisocki, P. A. (1977). The thought-stopping procedure: Description, applications, and learning theory interpretations. *Psychological Record, 1,* 255-264.

Environmental Protection Agency (2004). *Asthma home environment checklist.* http://www.epa.gov/asthma/images/home-environment-checklist.pdf

Everly, G. S. Jr., & Lating, J. M. (2002) *A clinical guide to the treatment of the human stress response: second edition.* New York: Kluwer Academic.

Federal Highway Administration (1995). *Highway traffic noise analysis and abatement policy.* Washington, DC: U. S. Department of Transportation.

Ferrari, J. R., Johnson, J. L. & McCown, W. G. (1995). *Procrastination and task avoidance: Theory, research, and treatment.* New York: Plenum.

Goldstein, A. P. & Keller, H. (1987). *Aggressive behavior: Assessment and intervention.* New York: Pergamon Press.

Greenwald, H. (1973). *Direct decision therapy.* San Diego, CA: EDITS.

Holmes, T. H. & Rahe, R. H. (1967). The social readjustment rating scale. *Journal of Psychosomatic Research, 11,* 213-218.

Hope, D. A., Heimberg, R. G., Juster, H. R., & Turk, C. L. (2000). *Managing social anxiety: A cognitive-behavioral therapy approach.* San Antonio, TX: The Psychological Corporation.

Jakubowski, P. & Lange, A. J. (1978). *The assertive option.* Champaign, IL: Research Press.

Karren, K. J., Hafen, B. Q., Smith, N. L., & Frandsen, K. J. (2001). *Mind/body health: The effects of attitudes, emotions, and relationships.* (2nd ed.) San Francisco: Benjamin Cummings.

Kleinke, C. L, Meeker, F. B., Staneski, R. A. (1986). Preferences for opening lines: Comparing ratings by men and women. *Sex roles, 15,* 585-600.

Lakein, A. (1973). *How to get control of your time and your life.* New York: Signet

Lercher, P., Evans, G. W., Meis, M. & Kofler, W. W. (2002). Ambient neighborhood noise and children's mental health. *Occupational and environmental medicine, 59,* 380-386.

Macht, M. (1996). Effects of high- and low-energy meals on hunger, physiological process and reactions, to emotional stress. *Appetite, 26,* 71-88.

Markus, C., Panhuysen, G. Tuiten, A. Koppeschaar, H., Fekkes, D., & Peters, M. (1998). Does carbohydrate-rich, protein-poor food prevent a deterioration of mood and cognitive performance of stress-prone subjects when subjected to a stressful task? *Appetite, 31,* 49-65.

Marlatt, A. & Gordon, J. (1984). *Relapse prevention: A self-control strategy for the maintenance of behavior change.* New York: Guilford press.

McKay, M., Davis, M. & Fanning, P. (1995). *Messages: The communication skills book, second edition.* Oakland, CA: New Harbinger Publications.

Meichenbaum, D. (1985). *Stress inoculation training.* New York: Pergamon.

Nadakavurkaren, A. (2000). Our global environment (4th Ed). Long Grove, IL: Waveland Press

National Institute for Occupational Safety and Health (NOISH; 1999). *Stress at work.* (DHHS Publication No. 99-101). Washington, DC: US Government Printing Office.

Noise Clearninghouse (2003). http://www.nonoise.org

Novaco, R. (1975). *Anger control: The development and evaluation of an experimental treatment.* Lexington, MA: D. C. Heath.

Occupational Safety and Health Administration (OSHA; 2003). Indoor lighting. http://www.osha.gov/SLC/computerworkstations_ecat/lighting.html. Washington, DC: Occupational Safety and Health Administration.

Rosenlund, M., Berglind, N., Pershagen, G., Järup, L., & Bluhm, G. (2001). Increased prevalence of hypertension in a population exposed to aircraft noise. *Occupational Environmental Medicine, 58,* 769-773.

Sauter, S. L., Murphy, L. R, Hurrell, J. J., Jr. (1990) Prevention of work-related psychological disorders. *American Psychologist, 45,* 1146-1158.

Schiraldi, G. R. (2000). *The post-traumatic stress disorder sourcebook.* Los Angeles: Lowell House.

Segerstrom, S. C. & Miller, G. E. (2004). Psychological stress and the human immune system: A meta-analytic study of 30 years of inquiry. *Psychological Bulletin, 130,* 601-630.

Selye, H. (1974). *Stress without distress.* New York: Signet Classics.

Smith, J. C. (1999). *ABC Relaxation Theory.* New York: Springer

Smith, J. C. (2001). *Stress management: A comprehensive handbook of techniques and strategies.* New York: Springer

Smyth, L. (1996). *Treating anxiety disorders with a cognitive-behavioral exposure based approached and the eye-movement technique: The manual.* Baltimore: Red Toad Company.

Surgeon General of the United States (1993). *Surgeon general's report on physical activity and exercise.* http://www.cdc.gov/nccd/php/sgr/atagan/htm.

United States Environmental Protection Agency; the United States Consumer Product Safety Commission Office of Radiation and Indoor Air (6604J; 1995). *The inside story: A guide to indoor air quality.* EPA Document # 402-K-93-007, April.

Van Kempen, E. E., Kruize, H., Boshuizen, H. C., Ameling, C. B., Staatsen, B. A., & de Hollander, A. E. (2002). The association between noise explosure and blood pressure and ischemic heart disease: a meta-analysis. *Environmental health perspectives, 110,* 307-317.

West, B. L, Goethe, K. E., & Kallman, W. M. (1980). Heterosocial skills training: A behavioral-cognitive approach. In D. Upper & S. M. Ross (Eds.). *Behavioral group therapy, 1980: An annual review.* Champaign, IL: Research Press.

Printed in the United Kingdom
by Lightning Source UK Ltd.
109264UKS00001B/92

9 781411 640689